JUSTICE
IN THE
MIDLANDS

JUSTICE
IN THE
MIDLANDS

How a Local Sheriff Solved a Thirty-Year Cold Case

LOU SAHADI

THE
History
PRESS

Published by The History Press
Charleston, SC
www.historypress.com

First published 2021

Manufactured in the United States

ISBN 9781467145428

Library of Congress Control Number: 2021934111

Notice: The information in this book is true and complete to the best of our knowledge. It is offered without guarantee on the part of the author or The History Press. The author and The History Press disclaim all liability in connection with the use of this book.

For Herman Young, who had fortitude and combined it with vigilance and dedication for justice in bringing closure to a small town in South Carolina.

CONTENTS

CONTENTS

ACKNOWLEDGEMENTS

My deep appreciation to Robert FitzSimmons, Barry Keesee, Robert Byrd, Tony Robertson, Ann Letrick, Walter Rutland, Betty McGinnis, John Justice, Joe Silvia, Julian Cameron, Mattie Caldwell, Johnette Freeman, Shirley White and Jim Stamm.

AUTHOR'S NOTE

I was visiting my daughter Elizabeth in Easley, South Carolina, when I became intrigued by a story I read in the *Greenville News*: a Winnsboro murder trial was set to begin after thirty years after the death of a local citizen.

Perhaps the suicide of a local man—a paraplegic—was instead murder?

How could a paraplegic move from room to room, collect shotgun shells from a kitchen cabinet, load them one at a time—although right-handed—and pull the trigger with a paralyzed left hand?

Why wasn't there a coroner's inquest?

And why didn't the authorities insist on an investigation with all the unanswered questions surrounding such a bizarre death?

I went to Winnsboro to find answers and interviewed a number of people, beginning with Sheriff Herman Young, a close friend of the deceased. When a trial date was established, I returned to the small hamlet of some three thousand to cover the trial.

1

THE PHONE CALL

K.C. Beasley will never forget the phone call. It came on a typical July afternoon in Winnsboro, South Carolina, hot and humid with the mimosas and crepe myrtles in full bloom, vestiges of summer's last flora to blossom. Only this wasn't a telephone call that Beasley at all wanted. It came completely unexpected, catching him completely by surprise as he was sitting on the front porch of his modest five-room house on Maple Street wiping the sweat from his forehead that only July's humidity can deliver.

That one phone call changed everything, changed his life forever. His wife, Eva, answered the phone when it first rang. All she did was listen.

"There's been a terrible accident," said the voice on the other end. "You better come quickly."

"Red," she called out toward the porch. "Hurry. Something's happened to Ron." Beasley got up and went inside, his handkerchief still in his right hand.

"What's the matter?" he asked. "They've called an ambulance for Ron," Eva replied.

Beasley shot out the back door and ran to his car, which was parked under the carport, fifty feet away. His only son, Ron (also called Red), twenty-nine, had suffered a stroke just three months earlier, a serious one that left him paralyzed. That's all he could think about, not knowing what was wrong. In less than a minute, he arrived at his son's tiny house on Forest Hill Drive. He ran up the five concrete steps and pulled open the screen door without any wasted motion.

Ron's wife, Sandra, her hand on her mouth, pointed to the floor. Red's eyes followed. He saw his son lying face-down, a rifle by his side. Red immediately looked up.

"What happened?"

Sandra just shook her head. Then, she began to cry. Finally, she spoke.

"Ron just shot himself."

Red really never heard her. He was kneeling over his son looking for any signs of life. He slapped his cheeks. Then he rubbed his hands. There was no response. From that moment on, Red's mind went blank. He couldn't remember getting up and walking out of the house. Or even how he drove back to tell his wife that Ron was dead. K.C. Beasley's world crumbled with that one phone call back in 1967, and he would spend the next thirty years trying to reconcile his only son's death—one he never once believed was a suicide.

It never occurred for a moment to K.C. that Ron would plan to take his own life. Not ever. How could he? In the first place, he was physically incapable of doing such a thing, holding a shotgun in his mouth and pulling the trigger. For all intents and purposes, Ron's stroke had left him completely paralyzed. He had use of only 20 percent of his body, and that was restricted to his left side.

How could he have done it? To begin with, his son was right-handed. It would take someone of considerable strength to position a heavy shotgun in his mouth and then reach far down the barrel to discharge the trigger. Ron Beasley, a helpless paraplegic, had nowhere near the strength. No, K.C. thought to himself, my boy couldn't do a thing like that. Something was wrong.

Beasley left without saying another word. He was too heart stricken to talk, let alone think. He drove back to his house without remembering that he had even left, maybe ten minutes in all. Everything happened too fast.

Even the short ride to the hospital was a blur. He vaguely remembered seeing the coroner, Earl Boulware, walking out of the emergency room of Fairfield Memorial Hospital. At that moment, he was convinced his son was dead because Boulware never looked at him. No one had to tell him Ron was dead. The coroner and a police officer walking alongside, told him all he had to know. They were convinced it was simply a suicide. The paperwork would be easy. Beasley had other thoughts.

This time, he walked slowly as he got out of his car. Eva was at the back door waiting.

"What happened, Red?"

"Ron's dead."

"Oh, no, not that. Don't tell me that. Did he have another stroke?"

She began to sob. Red held her close. He knew it wouldn't be easy to tell her he was shot.

"No." The word came out hard. "Then how?" asked Eva.

"He's been shot. I couldn't believe it, seeing him lying on the floor like that."

"Who did it?"

"Sandra claimed that Ron shot himself. Took a rifle and pulled the trigger all by himself. What bothers me is that no one tried to stop him. There wasn't anybody around except Sandra. It doesn't add up."

It wasn't until late in the afternoon that Red came out of his stupor, realizing that indeed his only son was gone. For most of that afternoon he just sat in his chair, looking at the floor without saying anything, listening to his wife sobbing in the next room. He finally got up and walked over to her sitting at the edge of the bed and held her hand. She just kept shaking her head, sobbing, "Oh, no," until Red stopped her ever so gently.

"I'm going back over to see Sandra and get an explanation to what happened to Ron. There's no need for you to come. There's nothing you can do now. And, besides, I don't want you to think of Ron in that house. It'll only cause you pain."

The house where Ron died was now alive with people when Red walked in. Besides Sandra, Mattie Caldwell, the maid, was there and so was Betty McGinnis, who helped look after Ron. Both were teenagers, and being so young, they couldn't understand what had taken place only hours before. Neither could Red.

"Now tell me how this all happened," ordered Red, looking straight at Sandra.

"Where's Eva?"

"She's back at the house."

"Let me come down and talk to both of you. She should know what happened."

Sandra followed Red in her car and within two minutes was standing in front of Eva, who was with Margie Perry, a nurse. Sandra began to explain what had taken place earlier in the day. She said that Ron had gotten out of his wheelchair, went into the kitchen and took some bullets out of a box, returned to his wheelchair and fired at her first when she walked into the room to check on him. The bullet, she continued, grazed her scalp. Ron then turned the gun on himself and pulled the trigger. It all happened so quickly that she couldn't do anything.

Margie looked at Sandra's scalp and couldn't find any signs of a wound. She glanced at Red and Eva and shook her head without saying a word.

Sandra made it known that the coroner ruled it a suicide and turned to leave without saying goodbye. She left without remorse, on a positive note, an official one that was marked suicide, and felt she didn't have to say anything else.

Like everything else that happened, the funeral was quick, too. Ron was buried the next day. Barely twenty-four hours after he was pronounced dead. There wasn't any time for mourning. Sandra had other plans. She wouldn't be a widow long. She would become Frances Ann Truesdale twenty-nine days later.

Herman Young, one of the pallbearers, who was a close friend of Ron, went to the house that night, just five hours after the funeral. He never went in. Loud noise broke into laughter, and he knew a party when he heard one. He couldn't believe what was taking place and didn't want any part of it.

Less than a week after the funeral, Red Beasley headed to the Pope Funeral Home on Congress Street, which was across the street from the country club, a two-minute drive from his home on Maple Street. An honorable man, Beasley was concerned about the funeral bill. Since the burial was quick and there wasn't any time for a wake, let alone flowers for that matter, he at least decided that his son should have the dignity of his bill being resolved so nothing could be said to smear his name.

"I told you to go ahead and bury Ron and I would see that you got paid," he reminded Julius Cameron.

"I'm sure his wife will pay it," replied Cameron.

"Well, I know for a fact that the insurance check is in," continued Beasley. "It's about $10,000. The reason I know was that I was keeping in contact with a person where Ron had worked. When the check came in, she called me and told me that Sandra picked it up."

About noon, Beasley received a phone call from Cameron. He revealed that Sandra had stopped by and gave him a couple of hundred dollars toward the bill. Red's voice got loud.

"What do you mean only a couple of hundred dollars?"

"She told me that she still hadn't received the insurance check and she wanted to pay a little bit on the bill."

"Sandra isn't telling you the truth. I know the check came in and that she's got it. Don't worry, I'll make sure that you get what's owed."

At about two o'clock that afternoon, Sandra unexpectedly arrived at Red's house, and she wasn't alone. Jerry Truesdale had driven her. Beasley didn't think much about it because Truesdale had been a frequent visitor to

Ron's home when he was alive. What occupied his mind now was the unpaid bill at the Pope Funeral Home.

"Did you take care of the bill with Julius?"

"I stopped by and gave him a little bit of money on it."

"Why didn't you pay it in full?"

"I'm still waiting for the insurance check."

"Sandra, you're lying. You have the check, and you already cashed it. If Julius isn't paid off in full by this afternoon, you're fixing to create a lot of problems."

Sandra began to hedge but didn't get anywhere and suspected that Red knew she had the money. She wouldn't get anywhere if she kept lying. She figured it was time to leave, returned to the car and drove off with Truesdale.

The funeral bill couldn't have been more than $3,000, and the insurance check amounted to $10,000. Red thought about that, and it perturbed him until about four o'clock, when Cameron called.

"Red, the bill's been paid in full. Sandra stopped by and paid the rest of it. Don't worry about it anymore."

Red found peace—at least for the rest of the day anyway. It didn't last. Betty McGinnis, who was still assisting Sandra around the house on Forest Hill Drive, called several days later and told Red that Jerry was making threats about him and that she didn't like the things he was saying. Red decided he had to do something, even if it meant a face-to-face confrontation with the younger Truesdale. Red was angry. He was angry enough to buy a gun.

He was aware that Jerry, as big and strong as he was, could destroy him if they ever came to blows. The gun he carried in his back pocket when he went to see Jerry gave him a feeling of security. He hoped that he wouldn't have to use it, but if he was forced to, it was there.

"If you have any problems with me, let's settle them right here and now," challenged Red.

"I've got no problems," answered Truesdale.

"I'm just sick and tired of all the talk I've been hearing, and I'm not afraid to do something about it," Red retorted

Jerry didn't say a word. Red left with the satisfaction that he told Jerry off. He never had any problems or contact with Jerry after that. What did irritate him was when Betty informed him that Sandra and Jerry had become lovers, and pretty hot ones at that, even while Ron was alive. His son had been dead about a week, and it was as if Sandra was dancing on his grave by throwing parties practically every night and making passionate love with Jerry afterward in Ron's own bed.

Red couldn't take any more. He was wired. He had to do something, and he called his son-in-law Dick Bane, a city detective in Columbia. Maybe he had a solution.

"Dick, I have to know once and for all, could Ron have possibly killed himself?"

"It isn't likely. What are you thinking about?"

"I'm thinking my son has been murdered and no one is doing anything about it and those that could have been involved are having a good time about it partying every night."

"I told you before there's not much you can do unless you want to get a warrant and risk not seeing your grandson Jody ever again."

"You're right, I suppose. But isn't there something that you can do? You're a detective, what would you do if it was your case and you had to conduct an investigation?"

"I never looked at it that way. Let me think about it and I'll get back to you."

Bane did more than think. In the week ahead, he decided to conduct an experiment. But first he had to recover the gun that supposedly Ron used to shoot himself. When he asked Fairfield County sheriff S.L. Montgomery for it, he refused to give it to him. Bane pressed him. He told Montgomery that it was Red Beasley's gun and he had no business keeping it without filing a charge of suspected murder. Montgomery didn't argue, and Bane had his rifle.

When he returned home to Columbia, Bane tied one of his hands behind his back with a belt and tried to load the rifle with the other one. He couldn't. He kept at it. He labored for an hour, sweat pouring down his face, and still failed. He couldn't put the bullets in the gun or cock the barrel. How could Ron possibly do such a thing with only about 20 percent use of his left arm? He concluded it was impossible, but he didn't go any further except to telephone Red.

Bane told his father-in-law about his experiment, which only made Red feel despondent and wonder even further why the police didn't push for an investigation. What were they thinking? This was no ordinary suicide. His son was paralyzed and helpless.

"My son was supposed to have gotten up out of his chair, which he couldn't because he couldn't walk, and went into the kitchen," reviewed Red for at least the tenth time. "Then he supposedly reached up on a shelf, brought down a handful of bullets, walked back into the living room, opened the gun case, took out the rifle and loaded it. The next thing he supposedly did was take a shot at Sandra and then put the rifle in his mouth and pulled the trigger to kill himself.

"What was Sandra doing all this time, watching? If someone aimed a rifle at me, and how in heaven's name could Ron lift and aim it, I'd certainly get out of the way and grab the rifle, from an invalid, no less. I don't understand the whole set of circumstances. I don't understand why the police just took Sandra's word for it."

Beasley was still trying to sort out Ron's death the rest of the week. He was completely convinced that Ron couldn't have shot himself and beginning to worry about his eleven-month-old grandson, Jody. He and his wife had babysat for him time and time again, and just the thought of not seeing him again troubled Red. He made one more call to Bane.

"There's no way we can get any kind of a warrant?" asked Red hopefully.

"It's no use. I did all I could. I met with Montgomery in Winnsboro and got no help, no encouragement. He told me point blank that the case was closed. He repeated in no uncertain terms that the coroner ruled it a suicide and that it was official and there was no use in trying to stir up anything."

And so Red Beasley was left with a painful memory: on July 6, 1967, his only son died. The pain was that he knew in his heart that Ron didn't kill himself, and what made it worse was that nobody wanted to do anything about it. What else could he do by himself? Nothing, he realized. Legally, he didn't have a chance. Bane's words were a reminder.

"If you want to see Jody anymore, you better not take out a warrant," advised Bane. "Let it ride a little while longer, something will come up."

Little did Red know it would take thirty years.

2
COTTON IS KING

At least eight times a day, maybe as many as ten, and all through the night, the shrill whistle of the Norfolk Southern engine pierces the quiet of the tiny southern hamlet. It appears as an intruder as it noisily rambles through Winnsboro on a winding track pulling nothing but freight cars, often a hundred at a time. It most certainly didn't rival the Orient Express on any of its memorable journeys from Paris to Istanbul. The old single track lies a block east of Congress, the town's busiest thoroughfare with a width of ninety feet, making it easier for the logging trucks to pass through the center of town. The railway has been there since before the Civil War, linking Winnsboro to Columbia. Cotton fields supplied the staple to the mills in South Carolina's capital. At the time, Columbia was the center of commerce filtered through the port of Charleston some eighty miles to the east.

The region and cotton were synonymous. In the antebellum South, cotton was king. England, with its endless textile mills, took every ounce of cotton it could as the most industrialized country in the world. Southern farmers could hardly maintain the demand. Even with an increase in growers, cotton remained a prize until diminished by the Civil War.

The cotton fields have long gone, with hardly a reminder that Fairfield County was once one of the leading regions for the crop in the South. John Porter, a tall, handsome stud with movie star looks, determinedly planted a field of cotton in the early months of 1996. It was a noble effort. However, an unusually dry and hot spring seriously threatened to dry up his crop before it ever had a chance to sprout. Still, he had plowed some 100 acres of field, some 125 acres of Silver Queen corn, along with another 100 acres of wheat, two sturdy crops he has done nicely with for a number of years.

John was a Trojan all right, putting in seven days of work, splitting time at the Porter Gas, owned by his father, Bill, and his crops. He would awaken at five o'clock every morning, drive his pickup truck to his fields some five miles outside the city limits and look up at the sky in the early morning light for a sign of rain. He was just about desperate enough to seek a Native American to perform a rain dance when rain finally fell the following day.

"The Indians have been the most mistreated people in our history," he remarked one Sunday afternoon before getting ready to repair his combine. His big red machine was a sight. It was over thirty years old, with wooden slats, a relic that nobody manufactured any parts for anymore.

His hope was Keith Peterson, a welder by profession, and he arranged to meet him at three o'clock that afternoon on the land that contained his cotton. He now had another worry as he examined the cotton. John discovered that the young leaves showed signs of thrips, and he would have to spray them within the next few days.

Keith being late only added to John's worries. He just shook his head as he looked at his watch. Keith was now a half an hour late, and John called his house to see if his wife had heard from him.

"Lenore hadn't heard a word," sighed John.

As he spoke, a pickup truck pulled off the road, which brought a smile to John's face. "That's him," he exclaimed.

Keith brought his Ram truck to a halt. A smile crossed his full bearded face. Along with his buddy George Hollis, who was sitting alongside, the two looked like they could appear on the box cover of Smith Brothers cough drops.

"Didn't think you was going to show," greeted John. "Told you I'd be here," answered Keith.

"You're a half hour late."

"That machine ain't going nowhere."

"That's the trouble. I got to make me a million dollars with it."

"You're liable to put a million into it," laughed Keith.

In a couple of hours, Keith made the necessary repairs. John climbed into the cockpit of the old geezer, turned on the motor and damned if the red monster didn't clackity clack with Keith's homemade brace. After a slight adjustment, the harvester churned with precision and never sounded better. John shut off the motor, climbed down and looked up at his old faithful band of metal.

"That name McCormick," he pointed out. "Isn't he the one who invented the harvester?"

"Cyrus P.," he was told. Today, he had Keith to thank.

The tall, rugged Porter sitting high on a tractor in the early morning hours forms a silhouette on the surrounding countryside, one that is lush with pastureland and forests with hardly any other signs of farming the red clay soil, which would yield bountiful crops if they were toiled. It is almost as if time stood still to a certain degree, with only the noisy intrusion of the train whistle breaking the calm air and not so gently either. Some environmentalist could make a case of an engineer leaning too long and too hard on his whistle as if in protest to the tranquility the area represents just I-26 miles north of the bustling capital of Columbia.

The whistles are like no other. They sound different with each passing engine, long and loud nevertheless. One in particular seems to affect the town's dog population, and they represent quite a number, too. It is a whistle with a high-pitched shrill that causes the dogs to jump and bark, some even howling with their heads pointing skyward, perhaps in protest of disturbing their sleep.

Porter may have been thinking of James Kincaid when he decided to bring in a field of cotton, which nobody had attempted to do in some fifty years. Kincaid was a large cotton grower and may have actually invented the first cotton gin in 1791. Although Eli Whitney was credited with inventing the machine, historians in these parts claim he stole the idea from Kincaid. If so, then Kincaid's wife should also receive some credit for the machine that made cotton king. Kincaid was out of town when Whitney arrived from Savannah, where he had been staying at the house of General Nathanael Greene's widow. Greene was a superior general who saved the South in the Revolutionary War. "We had been beating the bush and Washington is coming to catch the bird," Greene remarked at the time.

In her excitement over her husband's machine, she allowed Whitney to see it. He not only looked but studied it too, and he did so quite thoroughly. He, too, became excited, so much so that he left a lonely wife standing at the door, hurried back to Savannah, carefully sketched what he had seen and applied for a patent—all before Kincaid returned home.

Before the cotton gin was made known to the world in 1794, the town of Winnsboro had been chartered only nine years earlier on the petition of Colonel Richard Winn and his brother John, both of whom left Virginia, and Major John Vanderhorst of Charleston. Each had a command during the Revolutionary War, which had a somewhat dramatic effect on Winnsboro, although no battle was fought there. In 1780, British general Lord Cornwallis suffered a major defeat in the Battle of King's Mountain in North Carolina. Pulling out of his headquarters in Charlotte, Cornwallis decided to regroup his forces farther south in Winnsboro, arriving on October 29, 1780, and remaining there until the first week in January. It took Cornwallis fifteen days to complete the seventy-two-mile journey.

Cornwallis was indeed a gentleman with or without his powdered wig. He demonstrated as much when John and Minor Winn were among those arrested in a plot to assassinate him. Convicted at the trial, they were sentenced to be hanged. However, Cornwallis issued a pardon, perhaps as a token of gratitude for having used Colonel Richard Winn's house as his headquarters during his three-month stay in Winnsboro.

The war's end and a period of peace brought a number of changes to the town. The most significant was the erection of the Fairfield County Courthouse on the corner of Congress and Washington Streets. Robert Mills, a famous architect at the time, designed the handsome building, which is highlighted by four massive columns that supports the portico.

Just ten years later, downtown Winnsboro had another treasured landmark, the town clock. The tall, thin building that housed the giant clock, catty-corner from the courthouse, was stipulated by ordinance that it wouldn't be more than thirty feet in width. The whole idea of the building was to house the public market, which had been around since 1785. It was an upscale clock, too. Colonel William McCreight ordered the works from Alsace, France, in 1837, and the four-sided clock has run continuously ever since.

The only threat to the great clock, and to the stately courthouse, occurred during the Civil War. After torching Atlanta, General William Tecumseh Sherman arrived in Columbia and proceeded to do the same thing after sparing Savannah. The civic leaders in Savannah, which was a bustling cotton port, actually saved the city from the fate Atlanta experienced, dramatized so graphically in Margaret Mitchell's epic, *Gone with the Wind*.

The fabled general already had Winnsboro in his sights, determined to continue his burning there because of the railroad that linked the two cities, which heavily transported troops and supplies from as far north as Charlotte.

By the time Sherman rode into Winnsboro, all that was left for his troops to pillage were the hidden treasures they discovered in water wells placed there by frightened homeowners. They did so with alarming speed, no doubt from the experiences they had in Atlanta and Columbia, knowing they had to leave the next day. Still, Sherman succeeded in his objective of isolating Columbia from the rest of the Confederacy and neutralized the Confederate forces in the northern part of the state by duping them into believing that he was headed toward Charlotte sixty-five miles to the north.

Some one hundred years later, the law enforcers in Winnsboro would be duped by a spurious Sandra Beasley, who convinced the local authorities that her invalid husband had committed suicide right before her eyes.

3
WINNSBORO, SOUTH CAROLINA

The cool, sterile air in the first hour of dawn brought dew to the tailored grass on the final hole of Winnsboro's tightly landscaped country club. It is only a nine-hole course but a tricky one to par because the fairways aren't too wide, and it was far too early in the morning for even the most fanatical golfer to try. Only the rumbling of a noisy logging truck with its cargo of southern pine disturbed the tranquility of the South Carolina hamlet and with it the reminder that the town of some 5,600 inhabitants would soon be fully awake with cars and pickup trucks carrying them to work.

Ron Beasley used to be one of those workers in 1967, when Winnsboro's population was about half of what it is today. He never joined the country club or even thought about wanting to because he was too busy making a life for his wife and four small children. Besides, he wasn't the country club type. He was happy with tools in his hands.

There isn't much industry in this laid-back town, which seems to have done its best to reject the advances of the twentieth century by 1996. Oh, there are a few plants, but no major industrial ones that billow smoke into the sky. Mack Truck, Standard Products, JPM and Fuji at one end of town and HON on the other comprise the industrial segment. The nearest major highway is I-77, eight miles east, which offers a fast access to Columbia, twenty-six miles to the south.

Other than that, there isn't much more that M.C. Chappell, popularly known as "Snooks," who had been head of the town's Downtown

Development Association for the past ten years, can offer. By ten o'clock each morning, Snooks would know the luncheon specials of the day around town. He would walk to Yummies, Hoot's and The Tavern, on his own, mind you, and gather the information. A person would be wise to call Snooks and save making two other phone calls. More often than not he'd relate his findings to Janet Brakefield at the chamber of commerce in the clock tower building. Janet always went home for lunch unless, of course, she had a luncheon meeting, but at least she was equipped with the town's menu for any historical tours that were coming through. The signs at the city limits, "Welcome to Winnsboro, A Historic City," encouraged such excursions, although the tour business wasn't exactly booming.

Yet there is a certain charm to Winnsboro. Like all small towns of this nature, there is always a main street, only it carries the name Congress instead. Washington Street, which crosses Congress in the center of town, is the boundary line that identifies North Congress from South Congress, which seems odd for a street less than a mile long. There are no modem buildings on Congress, which is not lost on the young, just old store fronts and nothing higher than two stories.

Gary Brown's barbershop is there, Hoot's and Yummies, Price Drugs on one side of the street and Economy Drugs on the other, a couple of banks, three gas stations, the courthouse and clock tower building, a number of clothing establishments, with Belk's being the largest, the post office, far too many beauty parlors, two jewelry stores, a pawn broker, Cameron's Florist, Newton's Card and Book store, a converted gas station that is a Chinese fast food take-out joint named Speedee Wok of all things and Piggly Wiggly. Genesis Computer opened in 1995 and with it brought a reminder that Winnsboro was indeed part of the twentieth century. Although the post office closes every Wednesday at one o'clock even though World War II ended a half century ago.

The first person on the street as the morning light blinks on Congress is a white-haired Black man who sweeps out Pauling's Pool Room in the early dawn hour. Two doors away is the *Herald Independent*, a weekly newspaper that has been around since the 1980s, the last of three papers to service Fairfield County. Across the street, Terry and Cathy Rowekamp, two outsiders from Denver who opened Yummies in 1994, have the oven heating for the famous vegetable bread they serve at lunchtime. Slowly, the town begins to wake and, as usual, from a quiet night. The residents are proud of the low crime rate; an occasional drug bust in South Winnsboro, better known as "Mexico," causes the police cars to turn on their sirens.

The biggest thing that happened over the winter, which was unusually cold, was that Richard Winn Academy, a private high school at the far end of town, went undefeated in football and became Class A South Carolina champions. It was a long season indeed, as Richard Winn played twelve games, including the championship game itself.

The city's public school, Fairfield Central High School, three times the size of Richard Winn, had expected a big season. However, they got off slowly but managed to recover substantially, made the playoffs and proceeded as far as the semifinals before losing their run at a championship on the Class AAAA level. Between Richard Winn and Fairfield, Friday nights left downtown virtually empty, with almost half the town caught up in high school football.

When Ron Beasley was alive, the only high school in town was Mount Zion, a cumbersome building that occupied a square block on the east side of the railroad tracks, where some of the older houses from the Revolutionary War still remain. The Mount Zion Society, which was incorporated in 1777, founded the school. Although the society is still in existence, the school is not. It was closed in 1988 as a middle school, thirty-two years after Ron graduated.

In the fall, all of South Carolina is consumed with football. More so on the college level. Friday nights are reserved for high school action. The big day of the weekend is Saturday, and the majority of the college football fanatics around the state are divided between Clemson to the north and the University of South Carolina in the south. There is little in between.

Nothing is bigger at the season's end than the annual Clemson–South Carolina game, which alternates between Clemson and Columbia with each new season. At one stage of the rivalry, the game was so consuming in emotion that it was played on Thursdays. It truly earned special reverence back then, and the day of the week was hailed as Big Thursday, encouraging businesses and schools to close down in genuflection. Big Thursdays are no more, but the mania remains.

The front-page headline in the November 30, 1995 edition of the weekly *Herald Independent*, the local newspaper that serves all of Fairfield County, caught Blanche Robertson's eye that morning. As usual, she was at The Tavern for breakfast and, as usual, right on time. It wasn't an obituary this morning. Instead, the headline, "Justice to Seek Murder Indictment in 28-Year-Old Case," appealed to her but in an inquisitive way.

"They can't bring back a case that old, can they?" she asked. "I don't rightly know," answered Marjorie Dove shaking her head.

"They certainly can," offered Ed Arnette. "In South Carolina, there is no statute of limitations in cases of murder."

There wasn't much talk around town about the Beasley murder case. After twenty-eight years, nobody remembered much about it, and Sandra Beasley didn't give them much chance to with a burial in less than twenty-four hours. The younger people never knew anything about it simply because they weren't around back then.

Ed remembered it ever so vaguely. He was forty-six years old in 1967 and harbored strong opinions about the suicide. He didn't agree with the coroner's report. Arnette, a big Atlanta Braves fan, had coached Ron in Little League.

"He was a good athlete," remembered Ed. "A nice kid, too. It's a shame what happened."

There was no doubt in his mind that Ron was murdered although no one asked him about it.

"I used to work with his daddy at Fort Jackson for a time," continued Arnette. "He was really upset over Ron's death. He was convinced that his son was murdered and in no way could have shot himself."

It was odd that nobody talked much about the death of Ron Beasley back then. Maybe because it happened so fast. He was dead one day and buried the next. That hardly gave anyone a chance to grasp what happened. That's the way Sandra Beasley played it. And there was no doubt that it worked.

4
POWER BROKERS

Half the male population in Winnsboro seems to answer to the name of Bubba, and the town prides itself on being the county seat of Fairfield County. It may seem odd that a town so small could hold a mandate of such high esteem with the only telephone prefix being 635. It made dialing that much easier in that one only had to remember the last four numbers after hearing the dial tone, which certainly didn't help personal phone book sales at Newton's Apple.

However, it earned the distinction simply by being the largest city in the open, hilly county, which the Cherokee and Catawba Indians cherished as their hunting grounds before the early white settlers discovered its lush meadows. Winnsboro is a laid-back town of old money, but like all municipalities, large or small, it has its share of power brokers and any number of wannabes.

Quay McMaster had been mayor of Winnsboro since 1972 and lasted that long because he was a legitimate power broker, and no one dared to oppose him. His family fortune was accumulated in the gasoline business, and practically every Shell station in the county is owned by the McMaster clan. Quay would often remark that he made a fortune bootlegging gasoline during World War II.

As such, his power extended beyond Winnsboro and was present throughout the county, which numbered some twenty-two thousand inhabitants in 1996. He was a people person with a ready smile, always with a suit and tie and never seen without his cigar, which he ordered from Thompson's Cigars in Tampa. One could never figure how a Scotch Irishman could pass over scotch whiskey for Ancient Age bourbon, which was just fine as far as his wife, Lucy, was concerned. She abhorred scotch and would tell you as much, even without asking, and in no uncertain terms. Ancient Age for both.

A Friday night stop at The Tavern for the mayor and his wife was routine, usually around nine o'clock. Quay and Lucy would belly up to the small bar, and the bartender would automatically reach back in the shelf and pull down two bottles of Ancient Age. The bottles were miniatures, the same as they serve on airplanes. It didn't matter though. The glass was easily refillable, in as much as it didn't take long to pour out two ounces of liquor. They very rarely dined at The Tavern, and it was always Lucy who told Quay when it was time to leave.

"Quay, it's time to go," she would sternly remark.

"Yes, dear," he'd answer, and within a minute they were gone.

Quay loved his politics, and it was the season for it. The Winnsboro election that attracted the most local interest was the sheriff's primary. Herman Young, the one-term incumbent, was challenged by Leroy I. "Bubba" Montgomery, the son of Leroy Montgomery, who was the sheriff at the time of Ron Beasley's death in 1967 and no stranger to the office. Bubba had been sheriff back in 1992 and maintained the title for twelve years. However, his tenure was rampant with innuendoes and allegations that he wasn't always sober in carrying out his duties and, even worse, insinuations about his conduct.

Most around town felt that Bubba would get back in office despite the shadow of the past. For one thing, he was a good ol' boy, pickup truck and all, who had more political signs posted around the county than any other political candidate. More important, the feeling was that Young, although Black, wouldn't get the Black support simply because of the fact that he was hard on them. There wasn't anything negative on Young except that he attended more meetings that Bubba ever did and was at times hard to reach.

But Young won big, better than 2–1. His convincing triumph must have caused former senator Ellison "Cotton Ed" Smith to roll over in his grave. Back in 1936, Smith attended the national Democratic Party convention and was open mouthed when he saw a Black minister delivering the invocation. Smith was so overwhelmed that he returned to South Carolina the next day. Yet sixty years later, Winnsboro's Black and white communities came together, which Smith would have never envisioned.

Young won twenty-one of the twenty-two districts, losing his only one by a single vote.

The election primary the second week of June was of special interest to Quay. He was not being challenged, but Tim Wilkes, who had been the county's representative in Columbia the past eight years, was a protégé of the mayor and retired senator John Martin and was being threatened for the first time by Creighton Coleman, a local attorney with Kennedy looks. This was Coleman's first time seeking public office, and he was pronounced an underdog long before the polls opened. He ran a clean campaign and refused to engage in any mudslinging, which could have been easily initiated by a controversial full-page political ad that Wilkes took out in the *Herald Independent* proclaiming that Coleman had never voted in Fairfield County. Some of the voters in Gary Brown's barbershop voiced displeasure with the content of the ad, maintaining that it had nothing to do with the challenger's qualifications.

"Wilkes must be running scared to do something like that," said a customer in the one chair shop.

"Damned straight," agreed Brown, who still used electric clippers for his six-dollar haircuts and never once got caught up in the hair stylist syndrome of the 1980s. He was an old-fashioned barber, period, who happened to play a good round of golf.

He had the power brokers like Walter Brown and Spencer McMaster supporting him. Wilkes was still strutting like a peacock in being the only one of twenty-eight solons who was acquitted of taking bribes for voting favorably on legislation in the 1990 Lost Trust scandal, which rocked South Carolina politics statewide and left twenty-seven other legislators disgraced. The feeling was Wilkes certainly could swallow up someone with Coleman's naïveté. The political pundits made Wilkes a 10–1 favorite.

Wilkes never forgot his formative years. They left an indelible impression on him, not only his mother's courage, but also the warmth and love he felt in the years he lived on Vanderhorst Street. In the years that followed, he bought a house on Vanderhorst, near to the one he grew up in.

With a background of survival, Wilkes was conditioned for whatever challenges he encountered. The first time he ran for the House of Representatives in 1984, he won, and won every election since. But the biggest challenge he endured was the one for his political life, the 1990 Lost Trust scandal.

Five years after his acquittal, Wilkes collaborated on a book, *Presumed Guilty*, with Ben Greer, a teacher at his alma mater, the University of South

Carolina. The author, by his own admission, acknowledged re-creating dialogue "to achieve a more powerful sense of drama." He further confessed that he "did not consult courtroom transcripts of the trial but relied upon Tim Wilkes's recollection of his and other testimony."

That established the parameters for Cindi Ross Scoppe, who reviewed the book in the July 2, 1995 edition of *The State*. The crux of her criticism, in which she panned the book as "being too melodramatic," wasn't lost on Greer's vanity.

"The overwriting produces outright fabrications as well as subtly misleading implications," Scoppe wrote. "While wrong on inconsequential points, these repeated instances lend an uncomfortable sense of fiction to the entire account." She had more criticism for the unflappable Greer and the main character and didn't mask her displeasure at some of the passages she found repulsive.

"This is not a book that examines the very shortcomings of Operation Lost Trust," pointed out Scoppe. "This is not a book how the investigation changed South Carolina. It's not even a book about how the investigation changed the only legislator who was acquitted. Rather, it's the self-absorbed story of a smug winner who mistakenly believes that his acquittal suddenly makes his life story, including the color of his Jacuzzi and his fascination with coffee, thrilling reading."

What type of teacher Greer is was never explained. Perhaps he taught creative writing. His 133-page book was certainly an example of it.

What Wilkes attempted to do in his campaign against Coleman was to create controversy by at first questioning his challenger's political dedication. He chided his forty-year-old opponent by declaring that he wasn't a registered voter from 1982 until he moved his residence back to Fairfield County in 1995 after having lived in Richland County all those years. Coleman, tasting the first acidity of political stew, answered, "I always wanted to come back to Fairfield County, but it just got strung out." He maintained, "I don't think it is significant at all." Wilkes insisted that it was indeed.

"It makes you question if someone has an interest in good government and has always wanted to be an elected official, why didn't they at least exercise the privilege to vote," challenged Wilkes.

Coleman chose not to continue the verbal bashing. "He has elected to be negative on me to bring that up and I've taken the high road on this campaign," said Coleman. "If I wanted to be negative on Tim Wilkes, I could write an Encyclopedia Britannica."

Coleman was obviously referring to Operation Lost Trust and the freewheeling lifestyle of the forty-eight-year-old Wilkes, who finally married a month before the primary. Coleman, the son of retired circuit court Judge George Coleman, had been married for six years and had two children.

A Citadel graduate, Coleman earned his law degree from the University of South Carolina and spent more than six years as an assistant Richland County prosecutor. In 1991, he returned to private practice in Winnsboro. Before his run in the primary, Coleman got his feet wet in politics by working on several campaigns. The one of Barncy Giese, who was elected solicitor in 1994, wasn't lost on Wilkes.

Coleman was hoping that Wilkes's negative politics would turn off the voters. It was a classic contrast of styles, Wilkes, a New York street urchin, against a Citadel man of an aristocratic southern family.

A bigger surprise outside the Winnsboro primaries was the statewide one in which a couple of young dreamers, Harold Worley and Charlie Thompson, had the audacity to challenge Senator Strom Thurmond on the Republican side. The colorful Thurmond has been around forever, truly a living legend in South Carolina politics. While most people would experience difficulty in getting a job at ninety-three, Thurmond was amazingly still in public office, having served seven terms in Washington. And he was doggedly determined to remain there for at least another term. He was definitely George Burns's kind of guy.

The fact is, Thurmond, the Senate president pro tempore, was southern folklore beyond the boundaries of South Carolina. He achieved that status in the 1948 presidential election as the candidate for the newly formed Dixiecrats Party, which fostered state rights. His running mate for vice president was Fielding Wright of Mississippi. It was no national shock that President Harry Truman was reelected. What was surprising, however, was that Thurmond carried four states—South Carolina, Alabama, Mississippi and Louisiana—which gave him some kind of bragging rights to his great-grandchildren.

There hasn't been a more colorful figure in South Carolina's political arena than Thurmond. The state has produced some notable characters: Charles Pinckney in the early years of the republic, John Calhoun in the 1830s and, more recently, the one-eyed senator, "Pitchfork" Ben Tillman. Still, none of them served as long as Thurmond—even combined, which only magnifies the longevity of his tenure.

Thurmond's harshest critic was University of South Carolina professor David Lublin. He even termed the victory a weak one. And don't think that old Strom would forget it either.

Thurmond, in turn, got plenty of help. It came from Governor David Beasley and former governor Carroll Campbell, who rolled out their powerful political machine for Thurmond. He eschewed campaigning to attend his senatorial duties in Washington as head of the Senate Armed Services Committee. With Elliott Close's strong financial support, Thurmond would be forced to take the high ground on the campaign trail leading to the November election. Close indicated as much by quickly disclosing his campaign strategy.

"I think both Senator Thurmond and I owe it to the voters to stand side by side and face the voters and answer their questions on the issues we must address as we move into the next century," said Close, as if expecting Thurmond wouldn't be around by then. "We need to move away from the thirty-second sound bite campaign commercial."

For the first and only time, Winnsboro managed to savor a slice of national politics in 1964 when President Lyndon B. Johnson, who had been in office a year following the woeful assassination of President John F. Kennedy, ran against Barry Goldwater. In a history-making day on a warm October afternoon, the nation's first lady, Lady Bird Johnson, arrived by train as part of a 1,700-mile whistle-stop tour through the South. It was one time Winnsboro didn't mind another train passing through. An anxious crowd waited at the Washington Street crossing for the Lady Bird Special, carrying with it the sounds of the melody "Hello Lyndon," sung to the tune of "Hello Dolly," what else.

With the memory of JFK's tragic death still fresh from the year before, security was tight. Secret agents worked the crowd while some others appeared on the roof of Thespian Hall high above The Tavern. Pauline Patrick, the editor of the *Herald Independent*, worked the event as a novice for weeks, answering phones and typing on an old manual typewriter before she ever got into the newspaper business, out of Alton Hoy's CPA office. Almost a month later, Patrick received an attractive thank-you letter at her home in Greer with an autographed photo of the first lady and her daughter Lynda. The oversize envelope with "The White House" as its return address immediately caught Patrick's eye.

However, in the next instant she shook her head in disbelief as she noticed the envelope was addressed to "Mr. James Patrick." Apparently, women in politics weren't very big then unless you were Lady Bird. That was further amplified some two months later when Pauline received an official invitation for the inauguration of President Johnson addressed "Mr. & Mrs. James Patrick." She didn't attend. Not because of any impropriety, but her schedule didn't permit it. She still has the invitation, which is a conversation piece, in her house on Washington Street just two blocks from her newspaper office on Congress.

Just a day after the primaries, the poll in the November match-up showed Thurmond with a sizable lead over Close. Thurmond attracted 49 percent, Close 31 percent, with 20 percent undecided. This wasn't lost on Professor Lublin, who still didn't find Thurmond's latest margin convincing. "Anytime an incumbent fall below 50 percent, that's a danger signal and it should be a matter of concern," cautioned Lublin.

With his reelection, Young could continue with what he started in 1993. When he was elected sheriff for the first time, he promised that he would reopen the Beasley case. It would take time, and now Young had the time he needed.

5

ESCAPE FROM NEW YORK

In 1964, Herman Young was Patrolman Herman Young, a streetwise cop in New York City who operated out of Manhattan's Twenty-Ninth Precinct on Fifty-First Street and Lexington Avenue, far from the pastoral serenity of the South Carolina lowlands. The Twenty-Ninth was a low-crime, trendy midtown district of steel and glass skyscrapers, with only occasional robberies at fashionable Saks Fifth Avenue and constant traffic snarls surrounding the chic Waldorf Astoria marring a day at the Twenty-Ninth.

Young survived four years on the streets, but just barely. One night, Young escaped with his life, caught in the middle of a gang fight, left alone by his partner, who deserted him to fend for himself on a darkened street. It was a harrowing experience that remained fresh in his memory.

Young would never forget that one particular night. He was completely helpless and actually left to the mercy of the mob. The worst part was that he couldn't pull his gun. He was trained not to pull his weapon and fire any warning shots because someone could be leaning out of the buildings.

Young was out in the middle of the street, standing back-to-back with his partner, with only a nightstick in his hand and two gangs moving in on them from both ends. Suddenly, one of the gang leaders yelled something, and everyone pulled switchblade knives. Just as suddenly, Young couldn't feel his partner anymore. He quickly turned around and saw him running away.

Young was surrounded by two gangs, and all he could see were the flashing knife blades pointing at him. He didn't have any radio and couldn't call for help. His only hope was his weapon. He quickly pulled it out of his holster and shot one of the gang members in the leg. No sooner had he fired than a police cruiser flashed its lights, and he was spared. His partner did the unconscionable. He ran away and left Young to die. A little part of Young died that night.

The harrowing experience sent chills through the body of Young's wife, Peggy. She rebelled at the thought of being a policeman's widow. Worse yet, she couldn't envision their little daughter Keisha growing up without a father. That weekend as they were house hunting on Long Island, they stopped for a moment and looked at each other with the same thoughts. What are we doing, do we really want this? All the houses were close to each other, they all looked alike and there wasn't any open land. Is this the environment they wanted to raise their daughter in? It took a brush with death to tell them no.

Herman and Peggy were products of country living, and New York and Long Island didn't represent anything near that, nothing like the open acres, trees, sky, tranquility that shaped their lives. They could have all that if they left the city and returned to South Carolina. And Herman had the resources, a grandfather in Blair, just ten miles out of Winnsboro.

Young's grandfather Bun Thompson was a formerly enslaved sharecropper who picked cotton in the lush fields of Fairfield County, which produced more cotton than any other county in the state and most of the South before the Civil War. Although he could barely read or write, Bun was a savvy man and slowly began acquiring land. Before he died, he owned some four hundred acres in Blair.

"He always maintained that he didn't want the land to leave the family," remembered Young. And now Young, Peggy and Keisha were all going back.

Young was born in Blair, but at an early age his parents had moved to Sharon, Pennsylvania. His father took a job with Bethlehem Steel, and his mother worked in the munitions' factory assembling bombs during World War II to earn enough money to one day send Herman and his brother to college. After the war, they all returned to Blair.

Young eventually attended two colleges. He had no idea he would ultimately end up in law enforcement, never even studied it. At Voorhees College, a small Black institution in Denmark, South Carolina, he majored in electronics. He continued his studies at New York University and, on a lark, took the New York City policeman's test and passed. After four years on the force, he had enough of the city. There was too much country in him, and his grandfather's land was there waiting for him.

And so was Police Chief Marcus Ray in Winnsboro. Young met with him only once, and his police background in New York impressed Ray. He offered Young a job on the spot. Young was flattered. But something bothered him. He realized he was the first Black police officer in Fairfield County. Young was aware of the implications and challenged Ray up front.

"Do I have any limitations in doing my job?" asked Young.

"What in the hell do you mean by that?" Ray shot back.

"Well, I'm fully aware that I'll become the first Black man ever hired on the force."

"That's not a problem from where I'm sitting."

"That's all well and good, but…"

"But what, Herman, what's your problem?"

"Let's clear the air, and I'll put it to you simply. Am I going to be limited to just giving a Black person a ticket or if it comes to it, just arresting someone Black?"

"I hired you as a police officer. I just want you to go out and be that person."

It was barely a year after Martin Luther King's Freedom March in Atlanta when Young walked the streets in Winnsboro as a Black policeman. Young was prepared for the uncertainty. An outgoing individual, he had charm and charisma, and it didn't take long for the townsfolk to warm up to a Black cop with a ready-made smile and an engaging personality. He walked the streets and, every once in a while, twirled his nightstick, which he learned to do as a New York cop.

The kids hadn't seen anything like that before. They would come up to Young and ask him how he did it. That helped ease any tension that might have existed around town. The merchants became friendly, and they accepted Young as a person who had a job to do. That's all he could ask for. He knew he could handle the rest.

However, Young's days as a local police officer lasted only a year. He now had five years of police work and decided to explore job opportunities in the private sector. That decision was made for him when Ray left office. When he did, Young left, too. He had developed a close relationship with Ray and didn't want to work under a new police chief. From that day on, his life changed.

The first time Young ever laid eyes on Ron Beasley was in the Research and Development Laboratory of UniRoyal. Young had applied for a position and was immediately hired. And just as quick, he developed a friendship with Beasley, eating their sandwiches together at lunch. Never did Young imagine that it would last only a year.

From day one, Ron and Young hit it off just as natural as could be. In fact, they became close friends. Every day at lunchtime, Ron and Young would sit at a corner table, overlooking the disparaging looks from the other workers, and discuss such things as a design for a new part.

Young was amazed with Ron's mechanical skills, and he wanted to learn from him. Ron worked in the machine shop and was the best welder Young ever saw. Young was mechanically inclined as much as Ron, and that drew them together quicker. Ron was good at what he did, and he taught Young a great deal, too.

In the polypropylene department, they manufactured yarn for carpets. It was a new operation, and quite naturally, things were moving rapidly every day. Amazingly, Ron and Young came up with a new design to make the operations better. "He was good, really good," remarked Young.

The friendship of a new Black man in town and a settled white man nurtured outside the gates of the plant. Ron's wife, Sandra, met Young's wife, Peggy, and the relationship between the two couples grew. They shared dinners at their respective houses and did other things together, mainly attending car races. Ron was into cars and was an expert at building them, and Herman was right alongside.

Ron enjoyed cars probably more than anything else. He was always welding something. The two of them would rebuild cars for racing, taking the insides out and replacing them with aluminum so it would be much lighter. They'd even take the regular seats out and replace them with a single plain chair Ron welded to the floor. Ron was never happier.

One day, they bought a brand-new 426 Plymouth Hemmie from Doty Motors. It was a new model from Chrysler, and it was fast, very fast. It was so fast that there was only a three-month warranty on the motor. Doty Motors had to buy at least $400 worth of new tools just to service the car.

On some weekends they would go to different tracks around the state to compete. They had another buddy with them, Grady LeGrand, a state trooper. They took turns driving in the races and won their share of trophies. There weren't that many Hemmies around, and they were king of the hill with all that speed.

LeGrand was someone special to Young, but he died before Herman's election. When Young was reelected sheriff by an overwhelming 3–1 margin, LeGrand's sister sent Young a floral tribute. Young, Beasley and LeGrand called themselves the "Three Amigos."

There was one particular weekend that Young would never forget. He and LeGrand were to attend a race as spectators. However, they never made it inside. LeGrand pulled up in his car at the admission gate and left with fire in his eyes.

"I'm sorry, but you can't come in," remarked the gate attendant.

"What do you mean we can't come in, here's our money."

"Well, *you* can all right."

"Meaning what?"

In the next moment, the attendant pointed his finger at Young, who was sitting in the passenger's seat.

"He can't come in," He snapped.

"Well, if he can't come in, then I am sure as hell not coming in either," and LeGrand sped away.

The Three Amigos were indeed just that. Young's close relationship with Beasley was even more enduring. It flourished just two years after King's historic march. It might have not played well in the South. Nevertheless, Young and Beasley ate in each other's homes, worked together and did other things together on weekends. It was a warm, natural friendship, a Black man and a white man arm in arm in William Faulkner's storied South.

Young spent about as much time with Beasley as Sandra did. He even was a welcome figure at Mom and Pop Beasley's house, even more so than Sandra. When Ron suffered his disabling stroke in March 1967, it left Young in disbelief. He couldn't believe such a thing could happen to Ron, who was so full of energy, so full of life that he was always busy doing something. The stroke took all that away. There were no more dinners, no more building cars, no more races, no more lunches at the plant.

Yet the friendship prevailed. Young visited his stricken friend five or six times a week. He would walk through the house unannounced on Forest Hills Drive because he was expected there every day. For three months, he comforted his friend, who couldn't speak and lay motionless on a bed or in a chair. Occasionally, Ron smiled.

That smile told Young that Ron was glad to see him. He would look up and try to talk. He'd make a motion. That's why Young went to see him so much, hoping that his presence would encourage him to talk.

On one hot July afternoon, Young couldn't speak. He went to pieces when he was informed that Ron had shot himself. He was still in shock when he rushed over to Ron's house, couldn't even remember driving there. He looked for Sandra, but she wasn't there. The only thing he learned was that Ron shot himself with a shotgun and that Sandra was at the Pope Funeral Home making burial arrangements with Julius Cameron.

Young waited for Sandra's return. He wanted to learn from her how such a thing could happen. When Sandra finally appeared, she looked at Young and almost broke down emotionally. She sobbed that Ron tried to shoot her first before shooting himself, pointing to her head where the bullet missed. She mentioned that she thought Ron was tired of being in his condition and would rather be dead.

The funeral the next day was a blank to Young. He was one of the pallbearers but could barely remember what took place. His thoughts were rampant with all the good times he spent with Ron. Now he was gone, just like that. The stroke wasn't the finality, but Ron's death sure as hell was.

The night of the funeral, Young collected his thoughts. Alone, he drove to the house on Forest Hills Drive, where he had spent so many hours, to offer Sandra whatever help she might need. She was now a young widow with four young children to look after. Young never made it inside. As he pulled up in front of the house, he noticed several other cars parked alongside the road. His first thought was that there was a house full of mourners who had come to pay their respects. However, when he opened the door of his car and got out, he heard loud music coming from Ron's house. There was more. There was laughter and noise, the type that is prevalent with a party.

Sandra was having a party all right and carrying on. Young couldn't believe it. He couldn't take it. He cried for several minutes. He wanted no part of the gaiety, which he felt was a sacrilege to his friend.

"He was just put in the ground," sighed Young. "I just sat there and cried like a baby until it was time to go."

On the drive home, Young's thoughts gave him a sense of reality. His police-conditioned mind began to work. How could Ron have possibly killed himself? He couldn't move; he couldn't talk.

How could he get out of a lounge chair, walk to the back porch, reach up on a shelf, grab a box of shells, open them, walk back to the living room, take a rifle from a gun rack, load a bolt-action weapon, fire once at Sandra and then turn the rifle on himself and pull the trigger? And what was Sandra doing all this time, watching a helpless invalid and doing nothing? The suicide story didn't add up.

But as a young Black man who had already stretched social taboos, he wasn't in any position to challenge the authorities, least of all the coroner, who accepted Sandra's story that her husband committed suicide. He felt helpless.

When he arrived home, Peggy saw a troubled look on her husband's face. She sensed something was wrong.

"You're back so soon?"

"I never went into the house."

"Why not? You felt strongly about going."

"I just couldn't walk in once I got here. Whoever was there was having a big party, music, laughter, everything. I heard it from the street."

"I'm so sorry, dear. I know how hurt you must be. It's just so crazy."

"I'll tell you one thing, Peggy, right here and now. I will never forget what I heard about Ron's death and what I heard in the house tonight. If I ever get the opportunity to investigate Ron's death, I won't hesitate to do so. I'm convinced Ron couldn't have shot himself."

UniRoyal wasn't the same for Young without his friend. The memories were too painful. He left and opened an electronics business and never thought about law enforcement. However, he couldn't get it completely out of his system, and how could he help clear up Ron's death without being a part of the system? By 1982, Young was back in police work as the administrator of the Fairfield County Detention Center. He earned a reputation as an effective department head.

But he had one more goal. He wanted to run for sheriff of Fairfield County. In 1992, he easily defeated the incumbent, Bubba Montgomery, ironically the son of S.L. Montgomery, who was the sheriff at the time of Ron Beasley's death.

Young didn't forget Ron's death. After less than a month in office, he opened an investigation and made it his personal priority. He talked with Betty McGinnis and Mattie Caldwell, the two teenage witnesses who worked for the Beasleys but never interrogated, and became convinced that Sandra shot her husband in cold blood. It became more apparent after Young met Special Agent Barry Keesee for the first time in 1989. Keesee arrived in Winnsboro to launch an extensive investigation on Sandra Beasley, who had been Frances Truesdale the last twenty years, in the highway shooting death of her husband, Jerry Truesdale, in 1988. The more he talked with Keesee, the stronger he felt about an indictment of murder in Ron's death. On January 22, 1996, Young got what he was after all those years, a grand jury indictment charging Sandra Beasley with the murder of Ron Beasley.

But Young wanted one more thing, something quite traumatic. He wanted to exhume Ron's body to find irrefutable evidence, the bullet that snuffed out his life. There was only one way he could do so, and he needed K.C. Beasley's help. Young needed K.C.'s written permission to exhume the body of his son in order to conduct a forensic investigation to determine the path of the bullet that pierced Ron's head. It was a hard request to ask K.C., who visited his son's graveside practically every day. K.C. agreed without so much of a second thought.

"Just tell me what day you want to do it to spare me from going to the cemetery," he asked.

Young kept his promise. K.C. Beasley was sitting in his home on Maple Street when the unearthing began on an early spring morning in 1993. Young's anticipation wasn't without fear. He didn't know what condition the wooden coffin would be in after thirty years in the ground. His fears were allayed when the coffin was practically intact, even though the wooden vault containing the box had disintegrated.

As Young looked on, perspiring with emotion, lips clenched, the coffin was raised above the ground. Apprehension still remained in Young's mind. What would be the condition of his friend's remains? Carefully, the coffin, creaking with age, was opened. Young looked inside and was relieved that the skeletal remains of Ron Beasley's body were in a solid state. But the gruesome part was left. The brittle bones had to be delicately removed and placed in a body bag and transported to Newberry, twenty-eight miles to the west, for the vital forensic study.

Young managed to overcome any emotion that gripped his body later that afternoon in a Newberry lab as the bones were removed from the body bag and meticulously reconstructed on a long metal table. He wasn't sure he could handle the ordeal. He stood and watched for what seemed an eternity as the lab experts completed their study. When they were finally done, Young had the answer he was looking for. It had been buried with Beasley for thirty years. The bullet that killed his friend was a small caliber, like a .22. It was flaked and partially disintegrated and badly oxidized from its years in the ground. But it was a small caliber, and didn't Sandra always carry a .22?

Young was euphoric. But it wasn't over for him yet. It wouldn't be until he had his day in court.

6

HERMAN YOUNG AND RED

Emotionally distraught from the funeral and what took place afterward, Young was in no condition to report for work at UniRoyal the following day. He needed to be alone to reconcile the bizarre events, which all happened too quickly. The sudden death, a one-day burial and the laughter that night left him numb. He couldn't comprehend what he considered a heinous crime, one that snuffed out the life of his best friend. Never in his police work in New York or the year he spent on the force in Winnsboro had he encountered such an ordeal. But this tragedy hurt him more than anything because it cost the life of someone he called his buddy. As always, Peggy tried to console him.

"Why don't you just close your eyes and stop thinking about it?" she suggested.

"I tried, but I can't."

"I know it's hard for you, but try and rest. You hardly slept at all last night."

"How could Sandra do this to me, to Ron? I can still hear all that laughter and everything that happened after the funeral. There was flat-out no respect. My God, she buried a husband. Maybe I should have walked into the house that night and told her what I thought of her instead of sitting outside crying. But I hurt so much I couldn't."

Weeks later, a somber Young left his job at UniRoyal. It wasn't fun anymore. Not without his friend. No more lunches. No more talk about Ron's knack for welding aluminum. No more discussions on race cars. Even no more suggestions about what to do on the weekend. It was an empty feeling.

Young slowly ate alone, immersed in thoughts. The solitude grated at him. Some days he would find himself staring at his sandwich as if it wasn't there. He decided the best thing to do would be to leave because the memories were too painful.

No way he kept thinking over and over could Ron have killed himself. None at all. Certainly, there was no going back to the house on Forest Hill Drive. Obviously, Sandra didn't need consoling, not after the funeral night revelry, which Young couldn't endure and left him trembling as he sat in his car.

Oh, how clever Ron was, Young recalled over and over. He marveled about how good Ron was with his hands and how much he taught him about machinery that he never knew before. He thought about some of the good times with Ron and Sandra and how much they were into drag racing. He smiled when he remembered how he helped Ron by working on a new 426 Hemmie Plymouth that his friend had bought. He could see it all so clearly, as if it were yesterday.

"The car had only a three-month warranty and we covered up the tag so no one would see it," chuckled Young one afternoon in the converted two-story house on Washington Street that served as the Fairfield County Sheriff's Office, which he claimed was the most powerful office in the county. "Ron and I also built an orange Studebaker. He was really into cars. But the Hemmie was his pride. He was innovative enough to use a kitchen chair on rollers for the driver's seat. Once it does a wheel stand, it would just come back on the roll bars. We did that in 1966 before anybody else and now all the race car drivers are using it.

"That was some fast car. Ron painted on its side, 'Ron 51%, Sandra 49%.' Sandra could drive as well as anyone. She would go up and down the drag strip like a man. Ron and I would pull the hood, check everything out, make some adjustments and Sandra would drag again. She was very physical."

Two years later, Young purchased a 1968 Dodge Hemmie with a 475 cubic engine. It was bigger and faster than Ron's car, and Young had to wait three months after ordering it. And if he needed any reminder of his friend at the track, his five-year-old daughter, Keisha, would provide it.

"Get it, Dad, get it," she would cry out. "Red wants you to do this."

Hardly a week went by that Young didn't think of his friend. They bonded at a time when Black-white relationships in the South were looked on with disdain and utter contempt. Young and his white friend were oblivious to it all, even though their association was somewhat audacious. They never once looked at each other as being white or Black. And Pop Beasley and his wife looked at Young in the same manner. It wasn't until some thirty years later that Pop told Young that he absorbed so much abuse from people in Winnsboro about his being Black.

Young was impervious to whatever prejudice his union with Ron might have spewed. He just wasn't raised that way. Back in 1966, Young and his wife, Peggy, were still staying with his mom and dad. Young and his friendship with Ron and Sandra was never an issue. Both would often visit Herman and Peggy at their parents' home in Blair. And it was the same harmonious relationship when they were out in public. Two young couples, one white, the other Black, showing others how to have fun together.

Yet one specific incident, which occurred on a weekly basis, made Young uncomfortable. Whenever Sandra came to the plant to pick up Ron's paycheck, he noticed a change in his friend's demeanor almost to a point of withdrawal. In Young's eyes, Ron was basically like a kid being told what to do. Never once did Sandra ever ask Ron to go to lunch together. Young sensed that Ron was uncomfortable with the weekly arrangement of a wife walking in and grabbing his paycheck. He talked about it with Young and asked why he couldn't be like him and bring home his own paycheck. Ron's eyes looked at Young, asking why he couldn't have the type of relationship that he and Peggy had.

With that painful memory, Young left UniRoyal and took a position as an emergency medical technician at Fairfield Memorial Hospital. It was a new service, and Young was one of four persons hired, two white and two Black. A religious type, Young felt it was a message. Ever since Ron died, he felt strongly about wanting to help others. He thought about a spot like that, and suddenly it happened.

"Ron is gone, but maybe I can help someone else, other people who need it," he told Peggy one day.

Young sat next to the driver in the old hearse that served as an ambulance. He worked the same shift with Jimmy Terry. But instead of sharing the driving, he purposely let Terry drive 75 percent of the time.

"I wanted to help, be in back of the hearse with someone that was in need of aid," explained Young. "All the while I kept thinking about Ron. I felt that if I was around, nothing would have happened to him, that he'd still be alive. And, if I couldn't help him, then maybe in some way I could help others."

Young's new job gave him the opportunity. And caring about others gave him fulfillment. There was one incident in particular that he would never forget, one that he had to face head on without losing his composure. It occurred after he arrived in Jenkinsville to render medical assistance involving an automobile accident. Young was focused when he arrived on the scene.

"I looked for the person that needed immediate treatment," recalled Young. "It was a young white woman. Her father owned Carolina Meat Packing Company. She was badly hurt. I took out my scissors and began cutting away her blouse. She looked up at me and remarked, 'I don't have a bra on.' Ma'am, that's not what I'm thinking about right now."

She survived and so did dozens of others Young attended. During the time he worked for the hospital, he received many letters and phone calls from families thanking him for his help. Little did he know at the time that his unselfish work would help in his election as sheriff in 1993. And it was just like his parents always taught him, "You do what you can to help someone, and something good will come back to you."

And on his own, without any announcement to anyone, Young would reach out to help others. He didn't drink or smoke, and his reassuring, resonant voice brought comfort to the elderly. He would fix their light sockets, do some wiring, run errands and even drive them to a doctor's office. He was genuine, and his sanguineness touched everyone. Indeed, he was a man without color. Everybody's son, Glenn Boger would swear to it. Boger was an old disabled truck driver who was bedded down with the flu when Young arrived at his house one fall day. Young asked what needed to be done. It was too much to ask and too much to expect felt Boger. Young, with his infectious smile, left Boger in bed and went out and staked his yard and put up some fence posts that were badly needed. He performed hundreds of deeds just like that, and it took only a thank-you to fulfill him.

Young made it a mission to see Pop and Eva Beasley at least once a week. He was emotionally attached to both. Over and over again they would tell him, "You're our child. Red is gone, but we love you." That meant a great deal to Young, and many times he would leave teary-eyed. He would come and go any time, and always with a hug, in the Beasley's small house on Maple Street. He looked after them like the son they made him out to be. And Peggy was there, too. In her duties with the Council on Aging, she would have regular contact with the Beasleys.

But Young never heard from Sandra again. He learned of her marriage to Jerry Truesdale from hearsay, and it didn't surprise him. He knew of their relationship even when Ron was still alive lying hopelessly in another room. Sandra's stony silence troubled Young. He and Peggy were close friends, yet they never had any contact with Sandra once she left town. Sandra never called once since the night of the funeral when Young drove away from her house without ever going inside. All Young could reason now was that

Sandra had no love for Ron and all she was interested in was his paycheck. He still could not believe Ron had killed himself.

In 1973, Young had returned to police work. He applied for the position as administrator of the detention center where Sandra would end up one day, and for the next twenty years, Young diligently instituted prison reform. The detention center was converted from an old stockade that possessed squalid conditions for the inmates it harbored. It was totally segregated, and the prisoners were immobilized with shackles and chains. At night, the prison would rattle with the noise of inmates turning over in their beds with the sound of clanking chains.

Young eliminated the indignity of human beings shackled in chains like primitive animals. And he further introduced other reforms. He instructed his correctional officers to address each prisoner by his last name beginning with the title mister. He strongly believed that if you give someone respect, they would return it. The policy was strictly enforced, and it changed the inmates' attitudes. Young had a trouble-free prison that was a model correctional institution. His center never failed the twice-yearly inspections by the state prison board, and it didn't go unnoticed. Young's progressive changes earned him a number of citations.

However, Young's achievements didn't mean a thing to Sheriff S.L. Montgomery. Friction flared between the two because Young's model facility had become a deterrent to Montgomery, who had detailed prison labor for his personal welfare. Young was operating daily with a sword over his head waved by an old-time sheriff whom he looked on as a racist. Montgomery repeatedly threatened Young that he was going to take over the detention center and put him out of work.

Several years later, when Bubba Montgomery replaced his father as sheriff, Young for the first time began thinking seriously of running for the office. Bubba, who was a product of his father's environment, continued much of his father's practices. He also used vehicles that were confiscated and sitting idly in the yard behind the sheriff's office for his own personal advantage. As Young remarked often, the Fairfield County Sheriff was the most powerful office in the county, but it was being misused with no one challenging the illegal abuse. Peggy Young urged her husband that the time was now appropriate for him to run for office. He knew she was right. "Ron did not kill himself, and eventually I will prove it to the world," Young told her.

The first person to learn of Young's decision was Pop Beasley. Like a dutiful son, Young broached the idea to Pop and his wife. They encouraged him just like any parent would do. Hearing that, Young made them both a vow while looking at each of them in the living room on Maple Street.

"I promise you both that if I get elected sheriff, the first thing I'll do is reopen Ron's case," promised Young. "All of us here in this room know that Ron didn't commit suicide. Once I become sheriff, I promise you this case will come to trial."

Young was encouraged from the private discussions he had with Special Agent Barry Keesee of the Virginia State Police, who arrived in Winnsboro for several days in 1990 to interview several witnesses in connection with Jerry Truesdale's death. What Keesee confidentially disclosed to Young was the final convincer that Sandra, who would be indicted within months for murdering Truesdale, had also killed his best friend, Ron.

But Young couldn't lift a finger until he was elected sheriff. The office meant more to him, more than ever before.

Keesee's reports, which were submitted to the Fairfield County Sheriff's Office, gathered dust for two years; they went unattended in the files. Those same files would be at Young's disposal once he was elected. That's all he would need to launch his own investigation to reopen Ron's case. No way it was a suicide, he kept repeating to himself. And it drove him once he assumed office.

Young pressed hard. The only regret he briefly had during his relentless investigative pursuit was that Eva Beasley died before he could fulfill his promise to her. But there was still Pop. And that drove him more now.

"When Mrs. Beasley died, I thought to myself that maybe my pushing this investigation so hard created too much pressure on her," lamented Young. "God, I said, I did not push it. Once I reconciled myself, I stepped up the investigation even more knowing that Pop's health wasn't good."

Enlightened by what his investigation was turning up in regard to procuring an indictment against Sandra, Young continued his cemetery visits to Ron's grave site. "Red, I haven't forgotten you," he would whisper. "Hey, Buddy, I'm here."

The final visit would be the most traumatic of all. Young held up admiringly well the day that Ron's body was exhumed. What he discovered in the coffin startled him. It was a ring, too small to be Ron's. Young shook his head ever so slightly with the thought that at the funeral home Sandra asked to be alone with Ron. It was then that she placed her ring into the coffin, symbolizing that she was through now, reasoned Young.

But for Young, it was just beginning. Within a year, he would bring Sandra to trial, and Pop Beasley would be there to see it.

7

SANDRA

When Ron Beasley met Sandra for the first time, he had been divorced for about six months. He had been married to a Winnsboro woman, Gloria Douglas, when he was twenty years old and two years out of high school. The marriage only lasted that long, too. It was a shaky union. They appeared to get along fine the first year, but then, as Red put it, "she just went wild on him." Ron had enough, and a divorce was his solution.

He was working at the Shakespeare plant in Columbia at the time. He loved his job, one that made him feel wanted because they offered him a position. Ron was taking courses at nearby Midlands Technical School, and Red was proud of the way his son adapted and found some direction in the business world after a shaky year in high school. Ron had failed the eleventh grade at Mt. Zion High School and wanted to quit school when Red sat him down one day for one of the few father–son talks he had with his son.

"Now, you're going to finish high school," ordered Red, who was never known to be a forceful person. "I don't care if you're drawing Social Security, you're going to have a high school diploma. You might as well make up your mind to finish. It's not that you can't do it; it's just you don't care."

Ron looked at Red and shook his head in agreement. "I'll do it," he remarked, and nothing more was said. And Ron made Red happy. He applied himself, got good reports in the eleventh and twelfth grades and graduated. However, that was as far as it went. He wasn't the least bit interested in college like his older sister Barbara, who was quite a bookworm, the exact opposite of Ron.

Instead, Ron and his father decided that the next best thing was to attend Midlands Tech. Ron was particularly interested in machine shop, specifically welding. Red paid three months' tuition, and Ron responded by learning his craft. He learned it well, too. As Red said, "He was really into it." Red couldn't ask for anything more.

Halfway through the semester, things changed. Ron came home one day with a troubled look on his face, and Red sensed that something was wrong. His intuition was confirmed when Ron asked to talk to him privately. They walked through the house to the front porch. Once outside, Ron spoke first.

"Dad, I got a job offer today."

"Who from?"

"Shakespeare, the fishing company up the road from the school."

"Did you go over there?"

"No, not at all. They visited the school looking to hire, liked what I was doing and asked me if I would like to go to work for them. They said they'd give me a reasonable salary and guaranteed that I'd get better training than I was getting now. It wouldn't cost me anything, and I'd be earning money at the same time. How do you feel about it, Dad?"

Red pondered for a moment, his hand rubbing across his mouth. "Well, the first thing we'd better do is to see the head of the school and see what this is all about."

The next day, Red accompanied his son to Midlands. They met with the director, who happened to be a woman, and Red was surprised by what she told him.

"Mr. Beasley, let me say right from the start that I can't refund any of your tuition if your son decides to leave, and after what he's told me, that's a strong possibility. I'll be the first to admit that it's a good deal. He'll get a lot more training over at Shakespeare than he would receive here. And, for a nineteen-year-old, that's pretty good from where I'm sitting. Take the job and good luck."

It was at a bar in Columbia that Ron first laid eyes on Sandra. After his divorce, he and a couple of his buddies would hit some of the nightspots around the city. Ron wasn't much of a drinker, which was just fine with his friends, because it meant that he would always be sober enough to make the drive back to Winnsboro whenever they had enough beers. A dance was all that Ron needed to meet Sandra.

That's all it took. The next time Ron drove to Columbia, he was alone. He had a date with Sandra. It was the start. He had another and another, and they began seeing each other steadily. Gloria was now forgotten, and whatever bad memories he had from the marriage were gone, too. Ron was falling in love again with a woman who had three small sons ranging in ages from two to five. It didn't take long for Ron to ask her to marry him. It happened quite suddenly, and Red didn't know about it until it happened.

"Ron came to the house one day in December and told me and my wife, Eva, that he had gotten married at the probate's office," remembered Red. "We were in the backyard and Eva was standing behind a two-wheel utility trailer at the time. When he said that he was married, Eva pushed down on the trailer, and an angle iron caught her across her foot and broke three of her toes."

"We accepted it though. What else can you do? There's really nothing you can do about it, is there? He loved those three little boys as if they were his own. He never had any children from his first marriage, and the way things turned out, it was a good thing, too. Maybe that's why he loved those boys, maybe more than he did Sandra, or at least because of her."

Red didn't see much of Ron after that, not like before. But then Red never spent too much time with Ron when he was growing up. He was in the insurance business then and spent hours upon hours on the road. Still, his memories of young Ron as a child were good. He never had any problems with him except that one time when he failed the eleventh grade.

Only once could Red remember spanking Ron. He came home from working at Fort Jackson one evening when Ron was five years old and saw him in the backyard with a pack of matches trying to set the grass on fire. Red spanked him on the spot but never really hurt him. Red Beasley was not that kind of man. He was gentle and easy-going and was always good to his kids and wife. He had been married to Eva fifty-one years when she died in 1992.

Ron was raising Sandra's three sons as his own when she gave birth to a fourth son in 1966. This one was Ron's, and he was beside himself with joy. They named him Jody. At twenty-eight, Ron couldn't be happier. He had a regular job at the mill and did welding on the side. Ron was making money at both ends and working hard, maybe too hard. But he was young and appeared carefree, although he never completely trusted Sandra. After the experience he had with Gloria, Ron always wanted to know wherever Sandra went. Still, the marriage was surviving.

One morning in March 1967, Ron almost didn't. A young worker at the mill he shared a ride with drove up to the house to pick him up. It was a regular routine, five times a week. He waited and waited, but there was no sign of Ron or of any activity inside the house. He thought it was peculiar because Ron was always on time, waiting outside when he came by. He decided to get out of the car and look for Ron.

He knocked on the door of the small house on Forest Hills Drive, but there was no answer. He tried the doorknob and found it open. Once inside, he was surprised by the quiet. None of the children was even awake. He woke Sandra and asked her where Ron was. She didn't know. Sandra quickly got up. The first place she looked for Ron was in the bathroom. She found him all right. He was lying on the floor completely unconscious without acknowledging any of her cries.

She immediately phoned for help, and an ambulance transported Ron to Fairfield Memorial Hospital. After several hours, Sandra learned the grim news. Her husband had suffered a severe stroke, an aneurysm on the left side of his brain just above his ear. It was close to being fatal, and they had done all they could do to keep Ron alive and it was best if he was transferred to a larger hospital in Columbia.

For the next nine weeks, Ron Beasley lay motionless in the intensive care section of a hospital in Columbia. It seemed like an eternity. It wasn't something that Sandra bargained for, not with four young children to take care of. It didn't seem fair. Maybe, just maybe, Ron would recover, and everything would be all right again.

Miraculously, Ron finally did regain consciousness. But it was of little use. The doctors admitted they couldn't do anything more for him and that he would be paralyzed for the rest of his life. Sandra never planned on something like this. Now she had four kids and an invalid husband to look after. Sandra couldn't do it alone. Ron needed full-time care. She couldn't take care of him and her kids at the same time—no one could. She employed two teenage girls to help. Mattie Caldwell did the laundry and the housework, and Betty McGinnis looked after the kids and helped with the chores. It was all Sandra could do to survive. For how long, she didn't know.

In the months that followed, Ron never recognized his wife or his baby. The few times he spoke, he referred to Sandra as "her," or "that woman," and to Jody as "that baby." Only two or three times did he ever call Red "Dad." But there were never any conversations. Red and Eva would stop by practically daily, but it was to no avail. There weren't any encouraging signs about their son. The only way they could help was to bring little Jody back to their house to give Sandra some relief for a few hours.

This wasn't the life Sandra had in mind. Far from it. She was a free spirit who liked to party and have a good time. And she wasn't going to let Ron's condition stop her. She was still young, and men found her attractive. Why not have a party? And party she did. There were many nights like that while Ron lay in bed in another room completely oblivious to the world around him.

Red wasn't exactly pleased with what was taking place, but being the easy-going person he was, didn't say anything. People were beginning to talk around town, and it began to disturb Red. Finally, he had enough. He and Eva decided to talk to Sandra about her partying, but they were rebuked before they could finish. Sandra wasn't a person to talk to when it came to her likes and dislikes.

"I'm not going to clean up after Ron for the rest of my life," was the answer she gave them.

Little did Red and Eva know how prophetic Sandra's words would be. The final week in June, they were alerted by a phone call that Ron had been rushed to the hospital. It had nothing to do with a stroke. Instead, they learned that Ron had tried to commit suicide by slashing his wrist with a razor. Mattie Caldwell had heard groans coming from the bathroom one morning. She woke Sandra, and both of them found Ron on the bathroom floor, blood oozing from his wrist.

The explanation Sandra gave Red made him suspicious. She claimed Ron somehow made it to the bathroom, reached up into the medicine cabinet, grabbed a box of razor blades, opened it up, took one out and cut his wrist. He was stretched out on the bathroom floor, bleeding to death, when she found him. At that point, she immediately ran for the phone and called an ambulance.

Red thought about that. Ron was completely paralyzed from the neck down. What little mobility he experienced was limited to about 20 percent on his left side, his hand and his foot. How could his son possibly do what Sandra said?

Red didn't say much. He just listened. But he knew something was wrong when he left her. Then he remembered what Sandra had said several weeks earlier, that she wasn't going to pick up after Ron the rest of her life. That struck a note. If Ron was dead, she wouldn't have to. Oh, my God, that couldn't be it, could it? Ron would be dead by Sandra's testimony of suicide, and she would be free. She was a shrewd woman all right, but Red wouldn't know how much until about a week later.

Sandra began weaving her web. She started by creating such a disturbance at the hospital, demanding this, complaining about that, with such spite that the authorities wouldn't let her remain through the night with Ron. Somebody had to stay with him at all times, and Red didn't hesitate in being the one to do it for his son. First a stroke and now this. What else could happen to Ron?

Red spent the next three nights at Fairfield Memorial Hospital, sitting and sleeping in the same room with his only son, who looked lifeless. He had to do it because there wasn't anybody else. There were nights when Red couldn't sleep. Those were the ones that made it long indeed, when Red kept waiting for the first light of day. Long, dark, quiet, as if there was no world outside of that room.

Every so often, Jane Boyter, a nurse's aide, would sit and talk with Red. That helped, helped a lot. It made him feel alive, knowing that his son was lying in a bed half dead ten feet away, with his wrist bandaged, not even moving or saying anything. About three o'clock one morning, Red jumped out of his chair.

"Daddy."

"Yes, son."

"Can I go to the Y and play ball?"

"Of course, you can."

Red rubbed Ron's head with one hand and held his hand with the other. But there was no more. Just as quickly as Ron spoke, he fell back asleep. It was all so eerie.

But Red thought about what Ron had asked. He thought back to when Ron was about ten years old. He used to often go to the Tac Building where the YMCA was located to play basketball. Ron called him Daddy, like a child, and Red analyzed that his comatose twenty-eight-year-old son had lapsed back in time into his childhood.

That was a precious moment for Red Beasley. He didn't realize it at the time, but he had heard Ron speak for the last time. Within a week, he would be dead.

8

THE TAVERN

Before The Tavern closed its doors for breakfast, Blanche Robertson would park her gray 1989 Chrysler Reliant in front of the door on East Washington Street at exactly 7:30 every morning. One could set a watch by it. With *The State* newspaper tucked under her arm, she would nod good morning, take her decaffeinated coffee black and order her grits with a little bit of cheese and butter on the side. This was her routine six days a week. And she made sure she arrived at The Tavern first. On some mornings, she would indulge herself with two pieces of bacon but only if it wasn't greasy. And, on rare occasions, she would get a sweet tooth and cry out for some pancakes and only then if they weren't too big.

Breakfast was where it was at for Blanche, who had lived in Winnsboro all her life and worked part time at the Fairfield County Museum. She would sit at the front table and wait for her two breakfast companions, who would arrive within the next five minutes, giving her enough time to read the obituaries on the front page of South Carolina's largest newspaper. By the time Marjorie Dove and Ed Arnette joined her, they would know who had died the night before thanks to Blanche's watchful eye.

If there was such a thing as a breakfast club in town, it could have possibly started with these three. They had a leg up on anyone else if only by age alone. Besides that, they were fiercely punctual despite their advanced ages. At seventy-eight, Marjorie was the oldest of the group but not by much. She had been a widow for fifteen years and was partial to homemade preserves, the fruity kind, which she would spread on her single slice of toast every morning. Some of the jams that were given to her by her friends had some of the darndest names, old southern tongue twisters like Scuppernong, Muscadine and Damson, which would have been tricky contest breakers in a national spelling bee.

Miss Blanche was just that. She never married, and at seventy-six, she wasn't about to talk about it either. As one could imagine, being alone all those years made her a bit headstrong, which could be mistaken as stubbornness if you didn't know her. Simply put, she had strong opinions of things and people, and it took a great deal of persuading to make her think otherwise. Even then, she wasn't fully convinced.

Somehow, Ed, as he was affectionately called, wouldn't look right without suspenders, the kind with the metal clasps at the end. He wore them every day, along with his plaid shirts and khaki pants, and was fondly partial to baseball caps, too. He would change them every week and was easily recognizable behind the wheel of his twenty-year-old red Ford pickup, which he drove to Fairfield Hardware, owned by two of his daughters, six days a week. At seventy-five, he had been a widower for seven years and nurtured a strong love for Winnsboro, where he lived his entire life and wouldn't live anywhere else. As he was a deep-rooted southerner, strangers were all Yankees to him.

"There's a difference between a Yankee and a damn Yankee," Ed would always say. "A Yankee is one who comes south and goes back. A damn Yankee is one who comes south and stays."

Either one would be looked upon as an outsider. It's funny about a small town. Everyone seems to be related to someone. Kinfolk is how they identify it. It is a wise person who doesn't speak in negative tones about anyone. The bloodlines, dating as far back as the Revolutionary War, are firm and supple from one generation to another. It carried such a presence that caused one "Yankee" to remark one morning in The Tavern "that even the dogs in town were related."

And the town has its share of dogs, too. The remarkable thing was that none of the dogs that ambled along the quiet tree-lined streets was leashed or wore a collar for that matter. Surprisingly, it didn't present a problem for Winnsboro's Canine Patrol, which numbered all of two white vans. Much of the department's time was spent removing dead animals that carelessly got in the way of vehicles simply because they were old and couldn't move quickly enough. Dog fights, there weren't any that anyone could recall. Indeed, maybe the Yankee was right, and the animals were all related after all.

The Tavern, which served as the town's meeting place, was a beehive of activity when Polly Parker owned it. It opened for breakfast and lunch five days a week and dinner on Friday and Saturday. Patrons were amused by Polly's twangy stories as they waited for a table in the small, smoky bar.

It was a quaint establishment with a large, open kitchen. A rustic wooden floor defined the building's age; at one point it was a newspaper office complete with a printing press. During its years of splendor in the nineteenth century, a Thespian Hall for the town players was located on the second floor of the red brick building, which certainly made it difficult to act with a noisy railroad track alongside.

Polly was somewhat of a modern-day Ma Barker. She loved her bourbon and often carried her glass while greeting her customers. She had a following all right. A table wait on a Friday could last for over an hour, and the traditional Saturday morning breakfast could at times take a half hour. Polly wasn't always around on Saturday morning, at least during the early hours, depending on how much bourbon she drank the night before.

Her partner, Betty Gutschlag, was a quite bit more tolerant. She got by with white wine and needed every bit of her energy since she worked at the Fairfield Memorial Hospital full time. Between the two, they had cultivated a lucrative business—all cash, too, since they didn't honor credit cards. The Tavern was the only upscale restaurant in town, and Polly knew how to run it. Being the character she was, only embellished The Tavern's atmosphere.

The Tavern was *the* gathering place and did a brisk business on Friday nights, mostly at the bar, which was a room to the left of the restaurant apart from the diners on the other side seated in one of the four rooms. There were only six barstools around both sides of the black-paneled top that adorned the old wooden bar. The choice seats faced the door. They were cushioned and had arms, and it was a prudent reveler who got there early enough to sit in them.

The bar wasn't restricted to libation. Dinner was also served in the room, which could get quite smoky as the evening progressed, either in the four booths or a table that could seat as many as six that Bob and Linda Malone always reserved on Friday nights. They moved to Winnsboro from Maryland in the early 1990s and had no knowledge of the Beasley murder. A detailed individual, Bob would have reconstructed the murder if he was around back then and offered a strong opinion.

On the walls and above the bar itself, the room was decorated with ornate family crests. There were about three dozen crests to look at but less than a third of the people that owned them ever came to The Tavern regularly for dinner on Friday or even Saturday. Quay and Lucy McMaster, who didn't brag about a crest, preferred Friday nights, when most of the gossip stirred.

There was quite a bit of gossip on election night when Creighton Coleman reserved the Charleston Room for a party to thank his workers and supporters while awaiting the final results from the outlying areas. The vote was close, with the count in Chester County remaining to determine the election. Young Creighton felt he would do well there, well enough to maybe produce an upset since the race was so tight—wouldn't that be something?

It wasn't until midnight that the handsome attorney learned that it wasn't to be, that Chester County went to Wilkes. Yet his supporters were encouraged by the final margin of some three hundred votes. It was of little solace to Coleman. Citadel men hate to lose.

"Tim Wilkes will be looking over his shoulder for the next two years," one of his supporters shouted. It brought a smile to Creighton's face.

Red Beasley was well asleep by now. He didn't wait up to hear the election results. He wasn't much on politics. Besides, the politicians didn't do anything about his son's death thirty years before. It might have been politics back then when a coroner's report went unchallenged in listing suicide as the cause of Ron Beasley's death. Red didn't believe it then, and he didn't believe it thirty years later.

The question that kept appearing all these years was how could Ron kill himself? And Red's answer would always be there was no way he could do it. He was getting old and sickly and was too tired to do anything. All he wanted was inner peace. But it was hard. All that mattered most to him now, especially since his wife had died, was his grandson Jody. He was a piece of Ron, a Beasley. That's all he had left of Ron's memory.

Colloquy come easily in a small town. Winnsboro is that type of place. Everybody knows everybody else's business, which often makes for chatty conversation. It seems that nothing goes undetected in Winnsboro. Even the undercover cops can be identified, and it is a good thing the crime rate is so low.

Although not as sophisticated as Columbia, twenty-six miles to the south, or not that well recognized for that matter, Winnsboro nevertheless represents a vestige of the old South. It is reflected in that half the population are kinfolk and one has to speak softly on any subject matter that is derogatory. It's a cousinly atmosphere.

The residents reflect it in their beliefs. They share personal opinions with one another but would never go public with them. People had their own thoughts about Ron Beasley's death, but they would never say anything out loud. Some were fearful of Sandra Beasley, knowing that she always carried a gun. Mattie Caldwell and Betty McGinnis, the two domestic helpers at the

Beasley home and the closest to what went on there, never said anything. It wasn't until Sandra Beasley, who was now Frances Truesdale, was safely behind bars in Virginia that they shed their silence and spoke to the authorities to aid their investigation.

It is a big reason why people from Winnsboro are not conditioned to change. They are comfortable in their Lilliputian surroundings. Whether it's good or bad, they relish their separateness from the maze of modernization. It accounts for the fact that the post office closes at noon on Wednesdays throughout the year, shunning the outside world for a half day in the middle of a work week, valuing its seclusion from the rest of the universe. And any newcomer would be prudent to not even hint at the idea of change. In Ed Arnette's eyes, they are "damn Yankees."

Maybe that's why Ron Beasley's strange death went unnoticed for the most part. None of the authorities felt it was strange, consoling themselves with the thought that Beasley, as useless as he was, perhaps was better off dead. That was the popular notion, the easy way out. And besides, nobody outside of Winnsboro would ever know; no one would ever challenge a suicide.

Little did anyone conceive it would ever happen, too. Until Ann Letrick made a long-distance phone call one day in 1988 to Roanoke, Virginia.

9

JERRY TRUESDALE'S DEATH

The morning of April 21, 1988, was no different than any other. Or so Ann Letrick thought. She awakened as usual at six o'clock, got dressed, gulped down a cup of coffee and left for work in Columbia. She had been working at J.B. White's Department Store in the Dutch Square Mall as a hairdresser for the last two years. It was Friday, and she was looking forward to the weekend.

That single day changed her life. She returned from lunch and noticed something odd. All the workers were standing in the reception area crying. Ann thought that maybe something had happened to one of the girls' families, that somebody had died.

When she saw her two brothers and a sister-in-law, she gasped for breath. Before she could say anything, they told her that there had been an accident in the family and she had to leave at once. Ann began thinking that something had happened to her mother.

Nobody said another word until she got to the parking lot.

"Tell me what's going on," demanded Ann when they reached the car.

"Jerry's been shot."

"How bad?"

"Pretty bad."

"Oh my God, what are we going to do?"

She was beside herself. She and Jerry were very close, as he was the oldest and she the youngest in a family of four brothers and four sisters. She began talking as soon as she opened the car door, anticipating the worst.

"What happened? Was he driving his truck? Did he get robbed?"

The questions came one right after the other without waiting for an answer.

"No. He and Frances were coming back from Pennsylvania. They were on vacation and were heading home to Winston-Salem to spend it there."

"So, how did he get shot?"

"Somebody, they don't know who, ran them off the road near Roanoke, Virginia, in the middle of the night. They shot Jerry, but they didn't shoot Frances."

At that moment, Ann's mind went blank. She felt weak and didn't say another word. All she could think about was driving to a Roanoke hospital to see Jerry. In the condition she was in, she knew she couldn't drive, trembling with anticipation. As soon as she opened the door to her house, she went straight to the phone and called Dr. Roger Gaddy, telling him that it was an emergency and she had to see him at once.

Within five minutes, she was at Dr. Gaddy's office on West Moultrie Street. She didn't have to wait, either. The nurse led her directly to Dr. Gaddy's office.

"What's wrong?" he asked.

"Dr. Gaddy, my brother has been shot."

"What can I do to help?"

"I've got to drive to Roanoke right away. I don't know if he's dead or alive, but I've got to go there."

"Calm down, and take it easy."

"Please give me a shot or anything to calm my nerves so I can drive."

"Let's see what I can do. Maybe you shouldn't drive at all."

"I've got to see my brother. Dr. Gaddy, you're going to think I'm crazy, but if Frances was with Jerry, then I know she shot him. I just know it."

About an hour later, her nerves somewhat calm, Ann picked up her mother to accompany her on the four-hour drive from Winnsboro to Roanoke. She learned the name of the hospital that Jerry was in, but she didn't know if he was alive. Before she left, she called her husband, George, at work and told him to come home right away and look after the two boys when they came home from school.

Ann and her mother didn't talk much along the way. They were dealing with an unknown, except for the realization that Jerry had been shot and was lying in Roanoke Memorial Hospital. They didn't know how seriously he was hurt and how it possibly could have happened with Frances along with him. Not having any answers made the arduous journey seem longer.

It tore at Ann's insides as she drove north as fast as she could on Interstate 81, which took them to Highway 581 in Virginia. Finally, after what seemed like an eternity, she arrived safely at the hospital. She wasn't the least bit tired, flushed with anticipation at what was taking place inside.

She hurried through the door, and before she could find out where her brother was, she was approached by Jerry's oldest son, Randy, in the corridor that led to the Intensive Care Unit.

"Don't you dare ask Momma no questions," Randy warned her. "You let Momma tell you what happened when she's ready, you understand."

Ann stood looking at him silently, helplessly. Her mother was next to her, motionless.

"If you ask Momma any questions, I'll kick your ass out of this hospital."

That was the final indignity. She couldn't believe Randy would talk to her so disrespectfully, so threateningly. Wasn't that her brother in there? Wasn't that his mother who was standing next to her not knowing if Jerry was dead or alive? And no questions either!

She bit her lip to quell the anger that was inside her. She looked past Randy and saw Frances sitting on a chair in the corridor. Ann brushed past her nephew without saying a work and approached Frances. She knelt beside her.

"Jerry's been shot," was the first thing Frances said.

"I know, I know, but how bad and for God's sake how did it ever happen?"

Frances proceeded to describe the details. Ann noticed that Frances's legs were shaking. Frances explained that Jerry had been shot by two guys driving a car with a New York license plate. Then, a moment later, with her mother listening, she said the license plates were from New Jersey. Ann noticed the difference in what she had said earlier but didn't question it. She felt that Frances was traumatized by the ordeal the night before. It was all so sketchy.

Frances related that she rushed Jerry to the hospital as fast as she could, but he was near death. He was comatose but still had a brain wave as his only vital sign. She was going to wait in the hospital until there weren't any more waves on the monitor. Frances kept talking about how Jerry wanted to donate his organs. Ann never heard her brother mention that at all. She thought it was strange. And then Ann remembered reading in the newspaper that it was "Organ Donor Awareness" week. Was it a coincidence, Ann wondered?

"I want to see Jerry," said Ann.

"It's no use, he won't recognize you," answered Frances.

"I still have to see him," Ann insisted.

"But I don't want you to see Jerry that way."

"I'll be all right."

Ann walked ever so quietly into the dimly lit room where her brother lay motionless with the bleep of the brain wave machine the only noise. She reached the bed and grabbed Jerry's hand and began to speak in low tones.

"Jerry, I'm here. This is Ann. You were always there for me. Now I'm here for you. I'll do anything you want, just ask me. All my life you looked after me. Now it's my turn to help you. Tell me whatever you want, and I promise you I'll find out who did this to you and I'll make them pay."

At that moment, a tear rolled down Jerry's cheek. Ann was convinced that he heard her. Filled with energy, she left the room to find more answers. She was more alert now. The first thing she noticed was that there weren't any police around. Her brother was an apparent homicide victim, yet there weren't any law officers doing any questioning, any investigating. That troubled her, since her brother was shot just the night before. Surely this wasn't going to be another Ron Beasley case in which everyone accepted Frances's story.

Ann pressed on. She wanted to know where the police were. Frances told her that they had already been there and left. Ann was somewhat relieved, but far from completely. Everything was happening so fast, and nothing to that point had fully been explained. Ann wanted more answers. She wanted more concerning the police investigation and pushed Frances to continue with that part of it.

Frances began mentioning the name Barry Keesee, the police officer who was at the crime scene on Highway 581 the night Jerry was shot. Ann listened intently. This is what she wanted to hear, every detail. She got the feeling that Frances didn't like Keesee. Frances had told Keesee everything that happened the night of the shooting, but she wasn't at all pleased with his attitude. He had grilled Frances over and over and even checked her for powder burns. He even checked her gun to see if it had been fired.

Frances confided to Ann that she had bought a .38 caliber and didn't have the .22-caliber gun anymore. At the time, Ann didn't think it mattered which caliber because she wasn't into guns. However, months later it would play a significant part in implicating Frances because Ann remembered Frances telling her that Jerry had been shot with a .22.

Frances kept looking behind her down the corridor of the ICU, which was deserted. She cried out, "Jerry, how in the world could you leave me like this with only $25,000 insurance?"

Jerry had planned to retire from the Pilot Trucking Company in June and run a gas station that he and Frances had already leased in Winston-Salem. She claimed that she wouldn't get a cent of his retirement fund since he had died two months before it would kick in. Ann didn't like the whole scenario that Frances was creating.

Frances was getting tense and told Ann she needed to have a cigarette. She told Ann she could smoke in the stairwell, and both of them headed there. Ann insisted her mother remain seated until they returned. "Just in case one of the doctors comes by," she said.

She remembered Frances as being a heavy smoker and could see that the lit cigarette offered her relief. Frances began to talk easily and freely about the events of the previous night. She explained to Ann that she and Jerry had left Harrisburg early to begin their vacation at home in Winston-Salem because he wasn't feeling well.

They drove at night and were about fifteen miles north of Roanoke when they pulled their van over at a rest stop on Highway 581. While Jerry was in the bathroom, two men asked him for change of a twenty-dollar bill. When Jerry obliged, one of them confessed that they didn't have any money.

Jerry immediately left the bathroom and headed back to the van. The two men followed and continued to ask Jerry for some money. Jerry didn't respond. However, when one of them grabbed his arm, he wheeled around and punched him squarely on the mouth. The pair offered no comeback, and Frances thought that the incident was over.

However, about twenty-five miles south, the provokers passed the Truesdales' van in a Ford Granada. Suddenly, the car swerved in front of the van and quickly slammed on the brakes, causing Jerry to swerve into the next lane to avoid what could have been a rear-end collision. That wasn't the end of it. The car with the two strangers continued to harass them until Jerry had enough. He slammed on his brakes in the middle of the deserted highway and shifted into park with the intention of leaving his van.

Jerry was prepared for an all-out confrontation. However, before he could get out of the van, one of the two men walked up to the door and shot him behind the ear, got back into the car and fled into the night. Everything happened so suddenly that Frances couldn't think.

She thought that Jerry had been shot in the neck. He was slumped over on the passenger seat when Frances got out and took the wheel. She was frightened, not knowing if the assailants were waiting for her down the road. She told Ann that she wasn't running for help but that she was running away from them. Deciding there wasn't a hospital in front of her, she made a U-turn back toward Roanoke.

At that point, she reached for the citizen's band radio and called for help. It took only several minutes for an ambulance to pull up alongside. They took Jerry to Roanoke Memorial Hospital, but it was too late. Despite the paramedics' efforts, Jerry was too far gone. He was comatose, and Frances expected the worst.

When the police arrived, Frances described the two men as being in their early twenties, both over six feet tall with dark hair and military -tyle haircuts. All she could remember about the car was that it was an old, black Ford Granada with a New York license plate that began with the letters "RUD."

Ann believed her. But in the weeks ahead, that would change.

10

A WIDOW FOR THE SECOND TIME

Jerry Truesdale's funeral in Winston-Salem attracted about a dozen truck drivers from around the eastern half of the country. He was a popular driver who answered to the name "Lucky Devil" on the CB monitor. His luck had run out ever so quickly, so violently, dying so tragically at forty-one. Frances, who drove alongside Jerry on occasions, was known as "Big Spender." The name certainly fit. She was a widow for the second time, only this time she had $280,000 of insurance money waiting once the funeral was over.

Ann joined Frances in Winston-Salem the day after Jerry died. This time, her husband accompanied her along with her mother. Ann wanted to help with the funeral arrangements, but Frances tried to discourage it. She wanted to keep control.

"Ann, you don't have to go to the funeral home putting up with all that stuff," remarked Frances.

But Ann was determined. "Jerry would expect me to help you," she answered.

Ann thought she would possibly see Shannon Ivey at the wake. No one in the family, except Ann and her mother, knew that Shannon was Jerry's daughter. It was something that wasn't discussed because of one good reason: she wasn't Frances's daughter. She was the daughter of Frances's closest friend, Diane Ivey, and Jerry was the father. Shortly after they left Winnsboro in 1967 and moved to Columbia, Frances introduced Jerry to Diane. They were practically next-door neighbors, but it was more than Frances bargained for. Jerry and Diane got involved romantically right under her very nose. They had an affair, and when Shannon was born, Frances knew that Jerry was the father.

Ann didn't know about Shannon until about five years before her brother was killed. Jerry brought a photo album with him one time when he visited Ann in Winnsboro. She wondered what it was all about. Without saying anything, Jerry placed the album on the table, opened to the first page and showed her a picture of ten-year-old Shannon.

"Does she look like anybody to you?" asked Jerry.

"Not really," answered Ann, wondering what her brother was leading up to.

"That's my daughter."

"Jerry, you ain't got no daughter."

"Yes, I do. That's her."

"Don't joke around like that. She doesn't even look like any of us."

"But I tell you, she is mine."

And then he proceeded to tell Ann about his affair with Diane. He accepted the fact that Shannon was his daughter even though there weren't any blood tests made to confirm it. Besides, Jerry wouldn't question it because he always wanted a daughter. He loved her and supported her financially, and she grew up loving him.

"How do you think Momma will take it if I told her?" he asked.

"Jerry, that's your child, and it's not going to bother Momma. Gracious, what's Momma going to say anyway? She's got twenty grandchildren now and she loves every one of them. What's one more going to mean to her?"

Ann picked up the phone. "Momma, Jerry is here, and he wants to talk to you. I'm coming to pick you up."

When she arrived, Jerry showed his mother the photos and in low tones told her about Shannon. Ruth Truesdale smiled, knowing she had another grandchild to love. And protect, too. She never told any of her other children about Shannon.

All seemed to come together for Ann. She was pleased that Jerry confided in her, and now she understood why Jerry and Frances never stayed over when they came to visit, insisting that they had to meet friends in Columbia. That's where Shannon was, and that's who Jerry went to see. Being his only daughter, she was special to Jerry.

Frances pretended that it didn't bother her that her best friend betrayed her and with Jerry of all people. But Ann sensed that it was eating out her insides, not only at seeing Shannon but also just the mention of her name.

"We don't want none of these goddamn Truesdales knowing about her because I don't want them talking about Jerry behind his back," Frances vented to Ann after she learned about Shannon.

None of the Truesdales would talk about one another. They were a close-knit family and would help one another in a moment's notice. Frances wanted Shannon to be kept a secret because her pride was shattered. They wouldn't talk about Jerry but about how Frances's closest friend got Jerry to be her lover in practically her own house.

Ann realized that she was hoping for too much to expect Shannon to be at the funeral, knowing full well that Frances wouldn't even call to tell her that her father was dead. It wasn't Ann's place to call either, and she didn't. It was something between Frances and Shannon and she left it at that.

Before the mourners arrived, Frances demanded that nobody in the family was to take any pictures of Jerry in the casket. She wasn't taking any chances. Photographs can sometimes disclose things that weren't noticed before, no matter how small. She ordered the funeral director to kick anyone out who was caught with a camera.

This time Frances played the role of a widow just enough. That wasn't the case with Ron Beasley. He was buried in one day, and nobody had a chance to grieve. However, this was another time and another place. Frances knew that the president of Pilot Trucking would arrive from Harrisburg to attend the services for one of his drivers. There's a close bond among truckers, and whatever drivers were in the area detoured to Winston-Salem.

Only Frances didn't play the widow's role completely. Ann and her mother, Ruth, were the first to notice it. Frances looked sharply over at Ruth, who was crying over her son's death. He had survived the hell of Vietnam only to be killed so ruthlessly. He was too young for such a fate.

"Miss Ruth, if I ain't crying, I'll be damned if you're going to sit here and cry, so stop that crying right now," demanded Frances in one breath.

There were no more tears. Frances always seemed to get what she wanted. And when she raised her voice, people backed down, almost afraid. And Ruth Truesdale, like Red and Eva Beasley, couldn't do anything to offend her. It was easier to obey. Frances managed to show her some regard by introducing her to some of her friends, but little else. For the most part, she acted as if Ann and her mother weren't there.

Frances loved being the center of attention, and she was good at it, too. Until Clarence Crouch walked in. Frances almost lost her composure at the sight of him. He walked toward Frances and started to give Frances a kiss on the lips but bussed her check instead. Frances was beside herself.

Crouch had been the first person on the scene after Frances called for help the night of Jerry's murder. He was a security guard, a former cop, who had spotted Frances driving all over the road before she finally brought her van to a stop. When Crouch pulled up, he opened the door and saw Frances rocking a man, saying, "Jerry, I didn't mean to do it. I didn't mean to do it."

Alarmed, Frances cried out: "Don't you dare come a damn bit closer."

Now he was at the funeral parlor, and Frances couldn't believe it. She couldn't wait for him to leave. His appearance left her fidgety and nervous until he finally left.

"What in the hell is he doing here at Jerry's funeral?" asked Frances immediately.

No one answered. No one knew or had seen him before except Frances the night of the murder. He was trying to help, telling Frances that she had just passed a hospital. But Frances knew what she was doing. She was driving around and around waiting for Jerry to bleed to death.

Crouch was the one who called the police to the location on Highway 581. After the ambulance left, carrying a dying Jerry Truesdale, Barry Keesee and several other officers began their investigation of the scene. One, a policewoman, noticed that Frances had left her purse on the front seat of the van.

"I'll go get it," said the officer.

She never got the chance. Frances took off like a gazelle to recover the purse herself. There was something in it that she couldn't allow anyone to see. It was a .22-caliber gun, one that she was known to carry all these years.

The funeral was simple, and Frances wouldn't have it any other way. She didn't want any attention that would focus on her being the only one with Jerry the moment he was killed. Frances made certain that the preacher announced to those in attendance that Jerry had donated his organs. It was all part of her game.

She was playing her role well, especially when she spotted Big Al, as he was known, the president of Pilot Trucking. Frances jumped out of the lead funeral car in the cortege, ran over to him and gave him a big hug. Then quite calmly, she headed back to her car.

Ann thought Frances's actions were distasteful. How could she do such a thing? If you're burying your husband, are you looking up to see who is coming out of the church or walking on the sidewalk? That troubled her on the drive back to Winnsboro. She looked over at George.

"Honey, she killed him, didn't she?" sighed Ann.

"Definitely so," answered her husband. "She's going to get away with it a second time."

That sent a chill through her body. And for a moment, she thought about Ron Beasley. She was only in the sixth grade when the name of Sandra Beasley first made a profound impact on her. Her brother Jerry announced that he was going to marry the recent widow, which didn't sit well with Ann.

"You're marrying a murderer who killed her husband," remarked eleven-year-old Ann.

Jerry chased her up the stairs, and Ann made it safely to her bedroom. Not that Jerry would have hurt her or anything like that. Being the baby sister in a family of eight, Ann was Jerry's pet. In the years ahead, they became closer than anyone else in the family. It would be Ann who would eventually avenge his death some thirty years later.

Just twenty-nine days after Ron Beasley died, Sandra and Jerry Truesdale wed in a quiet ceremony attended by family members and a few friends. Sandra knew what she wanted. She had her eyes on Jerry even while she was still married to Ron. Ladies found Jerry attractive, but Sandra wound up with him. She told him she was pregnant and they had to marry. He was tall and dark-haired, well built, and had a way with women.

It wasn't long after they married, maybe several weeks, that Sandra and Jerry moved to Columbia to open a dog grooming shop close to the Shakespeare fishing pole company where Ron had worked. Sandra wanted a new start from her experience in Winnsboro with a paraplegic husband who first tried to commit suicide by slashing his wrists with a razor blade and finally did kill himself with a shotgun, according to her. No, Winnsboro wasn't the place for her and a new marriage, her fourth. She even changed her name to Frances to make the new beginning complete. And she wasn't pregnant after all. It was only a ploy, but she played it out to get what she wanted—Jerry Truesdale. She was attracted to him even while she was married to Ron Beasley.

"She wanted my brother the first time she laid eyes on him," remembered Ann.

Whatever Sandra Beasley/Frances Truesdale had, she used it well. She wasn't attractive, but there was something about her that men liked. And she knew how to use them to her advantage. Before she married Beasley, she had been married twice before. The first was to Maynard Lucas of Wagener, South Carolina. She was only about twenty at the time and gave birth to a daughter, Angel.

That's when Bill Fitch met her. He was from Winnsboro and was serving in the Air Force in New Bedford, Massachusetts. It was a torrid romance. He didn't know if Sandra was divorced and frankly couldn't care less. That's how much she affected him. They got married on October 17, 1960, and after his discharge, they decided to live in Winnsboro. Their marriage, happy at first, lasted five years before ending in divorce on October 8, 1965.

Even back then, Sandra was a disciple of deceit. When she married Fitch, she was known to him as Sandra Mitchell. However, prior to filing for a divorce from him, Sandra drove to Spartanburg, South Carolina, and took out a second marriage license in probate court and listed her name as Frances Ann Scott. She and Fitch were married for a second time on March 17, 1965.

Fitch couldn't understand why they had to get married a second time. Sandra Frances gave him the right answer. She explained that she wanted to get married under her right name for the sake of their children: Willie, Randy and Russell. Little did Fitch realize that she wanted it for the divorce she was planning that would take place six months later. Sandra had to be certain that it was a legal one.

After Jerry Truesdale's funeral, the next two weeks didn't go well for Ann Letrick. She kept questioning herself about her brother's death. Ann kept going over the murder in her mind over and over, at times talking about it with other members of the family. She was frustrated, knowing that something about the episode that Frances so carefully presented was wrong. Sleep did not come easy and offered no escape. Her restlessness started to create a strain on her marriage. Finally, her husband, George, spoke up.

"Quit talking about it and do something," he remarked.

But what? And then she remembered the name Barry Keesee. Yes, she would call him.

11

ANN LETRICK HELPS OPEN THE CASE

After she awoke the next morning, Ann kept repeating to herself, "I've got to call Barry Keesee." She kept reassuring herself because she was somewhat paranoid about him. During her two weeks of soul searching, she kept remembering how many times Frances kept mentioning his name, at the hospital, at her home, at the funeral and on the telephone that she thought Keesee was her accomplice in Jerry's death.

Frances had called Ann several times after the funeral. Ann learned that Frances sold the van in which Jerry was found dead within a week. She went out of her way to mention that Keesee was nice enough to take the van, which was covered with Jerry's blood, and have it cleaned.

After that particular phone call, Ann began to wonder. Why would the police clean up potential evidence before an investigation was thoroughly completed? Did Frances sell the van so quickly after the funeral to get rid of the evidence it may have contained? It seemed to her like the Ron Beasley case all over again so many years later, only a different town with different police. That's when she decided to take her chances and call Keesee. Yet she still harbored suspicions about him.

Instead, she placed a call to the Virginia State Police and talked with a Lieutenant Shields. She told him about the strange death of Frances's husband, Ron Beasley, when she was known as Sandra and that the outcome of the deaths were strangely similar in that both times Frances walked away without suspicion. Shields assured Ann that he would have Keesee call her in the next few days.

When Keesee called, Ann repeated her story. What bothered her, she told Keesee, was that Frances mentioned that he had checked her for powder bums and that he had also took the van and had it cleaned up from all the blood.

"That's a damn lie," snapped Keesee. "There wasn't any blood in that van for me to clean up."

It was all Ann needed to hear. She now felt that Keesee could be trusted and proceeded to tell him about the suspicious death of Ron Beasley years earlier in Winnsboro. It pained Ann to see her mother still grieving, and she was determined more than ever to not let Jerry's death go unsolved. No, she told herself, Frances would pay, convinced that she indeed murdered her brother.

Ann had to play it smart. Outside of her husband, she didn't let anyone know what she was doing. Most of all Frances. She couldn't have Frances find out because the phone contact she maintained with her was valuable. The more Ann talked to Frances, the more she could find out facts that would help Keesee reopen the case.

Frances made many of the phone calls to Ann after eleven o'clock at night, when the rates were lowest, and some nights they would talk until six o'clock the next morning, when Ann had to hang up and get ready for work.

In the months ahead, Ann kept up a front with Frances. And just as she hoped, she began to learn things, making notes of Frances's conversations that would be beneficial to Keesee. Her hovel on Gooding Street was going to be a clearinghouse of information, and Ann was dedicated to the role she assigned herself.

The more Frances called, the more exhilarated Ann became because she was gathering information that she could later relate to Keesee. Frances told Ann that she was cleaning out Jerry's sock drawer and found diamond rings hidden in his socks. Another time, she told Ann that some truck driver told her to go back to Harrisburg because Jerry had diamond rings on layaway in a jewelry store. She was freely spending the insurance money all right thought Ann.

Ann wasn't impressed that Pilot Trucking Company offered a $5,000 reward for information leading to whoever killed her brother. Jerry had worked for the company fourteen years, and certainly he was worth more than that amount of money. And besides, even an outrageous sum of money wouldn't bring her brother back. She dealt with the reality that his death was an uncalled-for tragedy and someone would pay. She was convinced it would be Frances.

When Frances told Ann that she gave all of Jerry's brothers cigarette lighters, she was surprised. But Frances quickly followed up, not wanting to offend Ann.

"I'm hunting something of Jerry's to give you, something special," Frances assured her.

"The only thing I want is a good picture of Jerry, one without anybody else in it," said Ann. She never did get one.

Frances began playing the impoverished role now. She claimed she didn't receive the $25,000 insurance money because the company was fighting her claim. She further cried that she had to sell her antiques, including the watch collection her father gave her. It got better. Frances moaned that she was forced to sell the Corvette that Jerry had given her, one she loved so much. Ann remembered that her brother gave her anything she wanted.

"I never saw a man worship a woman so much," remarked Ann. But she also knew what kind of woman Frances was. Frances was convincing. Even in a simple conversation, when she was wrong and the other person was right, by the time Frances was finished talking, she left the other person thinking she was right. It was an art form.

"She could convince you that black was white and white was black," said Ann.

Frances was not considered an attractive woman, but she was intelligent and a good conversationalist. She was tall and thin and was never without a cigarette or a mug of black coffee in her hands. "She couldn't live without coffee," remarked Ann. "She used a cigarette holder when she smoked, knowing it would attract attention."

Yet Ann had a good relationship with her. They went out to dinner often. They would go shopping together, and she recalled how her sister-in-law liked to visit old second-hand stores. "She liked being in another century," said Ann. "She was fond of old lace dresses like the older people wear. She loved stuff like that."

But if she loved Jerry and made him happy, that's all that mattered. She was clever at making matchbook quilts and often got as much as $250 for one at a yard sale. Ann could overlook the fact that Frances didn't cook much and never breakfast.

"Jerry would get up and cook breakfast every morning," disclosed Ann. "She didn't want to cook. She'd get out of bed when she smelled the coffee. She couldn't cook but she would sit down at the table and eat like crazy."

Whatever memories of Frances she had could wait. What Ann needed now was telephone conversations to write down anything she could that would help Keesee. Investigations took time, and Ann was taking the time to help in any way and right from the source, too. If anybody knew anything, that logical person was Frances. And the more Ann talked to her, the more she found how how much she lied.

"Jerry was better off dead," Frances dropped on Ann one night during a conversation.

"What do you mean by that?" countered Ann.

"Jerry had Agent Orange from Vietnam. He also had emphysema over 75 percent of his lungs, a severe hiatal hernia, five noncancerous polyps and scar tissue. He would have truly suffered if he had lived another two years."

Frances continued her litany of lies. She told Ann that she had talked to the man who got Jerry's heart. He had called from a hospital to thank her that he would get to see his two children grow up. How could Frances lie so much? Ann asked herself. Jerry's heart was never used. Ann wanted to tell Frances she was lying but kept quiet and left that for Keesee to do.

It took Keesee about a year to launch his investigation. When he came to Winnsboro in 1989, Ann met him for the first time. She was with her cousin Charlie Truesdale, a police officer. Ann wanted him to be with her for the taped interview. After some ten minutes, Keesee abruptly cut off the tape when Ann mentioned the .22 caliber. Ann was taken by surprise.

"She told you that your brother was shot with a .22-caliber handgun?" asked Keesee.

"Yes, sir."

"The only person who knew what kind of bullet was in your brother's brain was the Good Lord and whoever put it there."

"What are you saying?"

"Since he was an organ donor and they knew he was dying, they didn't touch the bullet until later, when they were doing the autopsy. What she was telling you when she said .22 caliber was that she shot your brother."

Ann couldn't believe what she was hearing. She had suspected all along that Frances had killed her brother in cold blood, but suspicion isn't fact. Keesee had confirmed everything she had felt in her heart. It was the first positive statement she heard that linked Frances to the killing.

The next time she met Keesee was at a welcome center outside of Charlotte on I-77. He needed something with Frances's signature to see if she or Jerry had signed his life insurance policies, and Ann had what he was looking for. She went to Columbia and obtained a copy of a deed of the house Jerry and Frances had bought in Columbia in 1967. She also gave him an assortment of greeting cards that her mother had saved with Jerry's and Frances's signatures, which Keesee took back with him to Roanoke.

The next time Frances called, Ann's eyes widened. She came right to the point.

"Ann, are you having me investigated?"

"What do you mean?" challenged Ann.

"Someone in the Truesdale family called the Virginia State Police, and they're investigating me for killing Jerry."

"Are you serious? Who would do such a thing? You must be mistaken."

"Oh, no. The boys and I sat down and talked about it and we agreed it had to be either you, Judy or your cousin Charlie."

"I can assure you it wasn't me. Do you want me to call the Virginia State Police and talk to Barry Keesee and tell him that's a bunch of crap?"

"No, don't call. I'll take care of it."

"Ann, I don't care if you tell her that I was the one who called. Just don't tell her that it was you because I don't want anything to happen to you," warned her sister Judy.

Ann realized that Frances's phone calls wouldn't be as frequent now, perhaps even completely discontinued. Since Frances learned she was under investigation and she suspected one of the Truesdales, it was prudent of her not to talk with anyone who carried the Truesdale name.

On January 23, 1990, Frances quietly drove to Winnsboro without anybody knowing and headed directly to the Pope Funeral Home. She caught Julius Cameron by surprise. He hadn't seen her since he buried her husband, Ron Beasley, twenty-three years earlier.

It was far from a social visit. She asked to see the burial records and told him she had been in Columbia and obtained a death certificate from the South Carolina Bureau of Vital Statistics. Frances intimated to Cameron that she needed the records for a lawsuit she had filed against an insurance company that refused to pay after the death of her husband, Jerry Truesdale, on April 23, 1988.

Frances's memory was lucid. She related details about Ron's attempt at suicide by cutting his wrists in 1967. She then reminded Cameron that he was the one who took Ron to the hospital and brought him home a few days later. She even recalled to Cameron that he was the one who removed the stitches out of Ron's neck after he killed himself and before he was buried.

After leaving Cameron, Frances drove to Coroner Joe Silvia's office to obtain a copy of the death report. She was furnished with a copy of the handwritten report compiled by Earl Boulware, who labeled Ron's death a suicide. After glancing at it, she commented to Silvia that it didn't look like a legal document in her eyes and probably not to anybody else.

She repeated to Silvia that she needed the document in connection with a lawsuit she had filed against an insurance company that refused to pay her on the murder of her husband, Jerry Truesdale. Frances was convincing. She impressed on Silvia that her lawyer needed to get legal documents connected to Ron's death because someone had started malicious rumors about how he died. Before she left, she asked Silvia to keep her visit confidential because she didn't want the Truesdale family to know she was in Winnsboro.

Before returning to Winston-Salem, Frances made one more stop. Eva and Red Beasley were the next ones taken by surprise, and Frances weaved another tale. She told them she was riding down I-77 when she decided to come by and visit them. She never mentioned that she stopped at the Pope Funeral Home or the coroner's office.

The visit was not exactly a social one either. Frances had a reason. She asked if anyone was inquiring about Ron's death but didn't get an answer. Frances was looking for any information that would benefit her coverup on the pending investigation. Her final words to the Beasleys were not to tell any of the Truesdales that she had been in town. Frances was covering her tracks.

12

BARRY KEESEE WAS CONVINCED

Barry Keesee was on a mission. He couldn't expect any more help from Ann Letrick. She supplied him with all the information she culled from her conversations with Frances Truesdale, and he was thankful for that. Now the rest was up to him, and he was good at what he did. Keesee had been in police work for twenty-three years, and it was left up to him to sort out all the information and go from there. He felt he had enough facts to produce an indictment in the murder of Jerry Truesdale. He was convinced it was Frances, who masqueraded as the forlorn widow in desperate financial straits. It would take him two years to succeed. And he had to start with the persona of Sandra Beasley to do so.

He arrived in Winnsboro the night of November 19, 1989, to prepare for his first interview the next morning with Eva and Red Beasley. Although their only son allegedly killed himself twenty-two years earlier, the memory of his death was still painful to them. But there wasn't any investigation done at the time, and they were more than agreeable to cooperate with one now.

They spoke slowly and carefully about the events as they knew them. Red revealed that Sandra told him that Ron asked her to bring him the gun. He was supposed to be sitting in a chair in the living room, and Sandra went into another part of the house to retrieve a .22 automatic rifle, one that Red had actually given him. Sandra claimed she checked the rifle and it wasn't loaded. She then gave Ron the rifle and left the room.

A few minutes later, as she was coming out of the bathroom, he shot at her. Sandra said she crawled out of the back door and he then loaded the rifle, put it to his mouth and killed himself. She went as far as to tell Eva Beasley that her son shot at her twice and that the two bullets he fired at her were so close to her head that they went through her hair.

Eva Beasley said that Sandra and Ron used to target practice frequently with rifles and she would brag about how much of a better shot she was than Ron. One day when she was at their house on Forest Hills Drive, Sandra was standing at the back door with a pistol in her hand. In the next moment, she aimed at a ditch about thirty yards away and killed a big field rat with a single shot.

The Beasleys grew more emotional when Keesee questioned them about Ron's attempt at suicide the week before the shooting incident. Their son was completely paralyzed on the right side, yet his left wrist and the left side of his throat had been cut.

Sandra told Eva Beasley that Ron had gotten out of bed on this particular night, made his way into the bathroom and grabbed the razor blade off the side of the tub. She said she had shaved her legs the night before, taken the blade out of the razor and left it on the tub.

However, both agreed that there was no doubt in their minds that their son was not capable of killing himself. His physical and mental capacities alone wouldn't have permitted it. Ron's mental state was that of a twelve- or thirteen-year-old boy.

"The story about him cutting his wrist and throat as told by Sandra would have been impossible and is totally a lie," exclaimed Beasley. The next thing Red said caught Keesee's attention. While his son was in the hospital, Sandra stopped by.

"She said that she was sick and tired of taking care of Ron and knew a way out of it," disclosed Red.

Keesee learned more than he expected. Eva Beasley furnished him with a distressing admission, one from Betty Ruth McGinnis, who was living with Ron and Sandra at the time of Ron's demise. Betty Ruth disclosed to the Beasleys that Jerry Truesdale was dating Sandra shortly after her son's stroke and even stayed at the house on occasion. What's more, they went out dancing after the funeral.

It puzzled Keesee why there wasn't any investigation conducted with all that he was hearing, of all the suspicious circumstances before and after Ron Beasley's death. When he asked Eva and Red about it, they broke down and cried. It was time for Keesee to leave, and he headed to his next appointment.

Keesee drove to 501 North Vanderhorst Street to interview Betty Ruth McGinnis at her home. She also happened to be the first cousin of Jerry

Truesdale. She had lived with Sandra and Ron Beasley from March 1967 to July to help take care of the children after Ron suffered his paralyzing stroke. Keesee wanted to know about Ron's suicide attempt on July 1 of that year, and Betty Ruth told him.

She had been asleep on the living room sofa when she was awakened by moans coming from Ron's room. She immediately got up and started toward the room when she was stopped by Sandra, surprised at seeing her, who was fully dressed.

"Don't open the door to his room," ordered Sandra. "Ron tried to kill himself."

Betty Ruth was stunned by Sandra's attitude. She didn't appear upset in the least and didn't telephone for help until both walked into Ron's room. It was only then that Sandra explained that Ron's bed was covered with blood because he tried to kill himself with a razor.

She didn't believe it. "Ron couldn't walk or get around by himself," remarked Betty Ruth. "He was completely helpless when it came to controlling his bladder or bowel movements and had to wear a diaper."

She didn't believe it either when Keesee informed her he had been told by someone else that Ron had gotten out of his bed, made his way to the bathroom, got a razor blade from the edge of the tub, made his way back to his bed and cut his wrist.

"In his physical and mental state, it would have been impossible," remarked Betty Ruth. Keesee wanted to learn more about the events of July 6. Betty Ruth vividly remembered that Sandra insisted that she go to the store and take one of the kids with her on that particular morning. She sensed that Sandra wanted her out of the house. She didn't argue.

Instead, she jumped in Ron's pickup truck and pulled up at the Collins Market on Ninth Street and Columbia Road. From there, she drove over to her father's house only to learn that Ron had shot himself. It couldn't be, she said to herself. She had been gone only an hour. When Betty Ruth arrived back at the house, Sandra claimed that Ron killed himself without going into any details.

Then Betty Ruth told Keesee something else that he found interesting. She was walking down the street a few days after Ron had died when Sandra approached her with a stem warning. She told Betty Ruth that she heard that people were saying that she shot Ron. In so many words, Sandra told Betty Ruth that if she heard any more of that talk, she would start doing some shooting. Betty Ruth was frightened. She knew that Sandra carried a handgun in her pocketbook at all times.

Tuesday, November 21, 1989, was a busy one for Keesee as he arranged interviews. His first was with Julius Cameron. Besides being the funeral director at the Pope Funeral Home, Julius was a personal friend of Ron Beasley's and transported him on numerous occasions after he had his stroke.

Cameron confirmed that Ron's mental state at the time of death was that of a young child. When Cameron prepared Ron for embalming, he discovered that he was wearing diapers. He felt that Ron didn't know him when he was alive even though they grew up together and attended the same school. At one point after he was stricken, his friend couldn't move either his hands or his feet.

Cameron explained that Ron had a difficult time talking, and when he did, no one could understand him. Then he volunteered his own opinion, both as an ambulance attendant and a funeral director. "Ron was physically unable to handle the rifle to shoot at his wife or take his own life," said Cameron.

"Sandra was a very smart woman and trying to get ahead of her was a hard thing to do," said Bill Fitch.

Keesee's final interview of the day was with Barbara Martin, a registered nurse. It wasn't a long interview, but it was beneficial because it confirmed that Sandra always had a gun in her possession. Martin remembered Frances Truesdale as Sandra Fitch when she worked in the Fairfield County Hospital as a candy striper during the spring of 1965 when she was sixteen years old.

"Sandra was in traction as the result of an automobile wreck and couldn't reach her pocketbook on the floor," remembered Barbara. "I reached down and got the pocketbook and noticed a small handgun inside. I was shocked and asked her why she had a gun in her pocketbook inside of a hospital of all places. She said something to the effect that she needed to have something for protection."

Keesee was pleased. After two days of interviews, he was constructing a case against Frances Scott Truesdale, also known as Sandra, prior to her marriage to Ron Beasley. He returned to Salem, Virginia, to start putting the pieces together that would link Frances Truesdale to the cold-blooded murder of her husband. He was buoyed by what he discovered about her in Winnsboro, where she was known to everyone who was in contact with her as Sandra.

Keesee didn't return to Winnsboro until November 30, 1989. He was troubled by the fact that there wasn't any investigation conducted following Ron Beasley's suspicious suicide. A paraplegic shooting himself was impossible he thought. And he had statements from others that indicated so and quite vehemently at that. But why no investigation?

Keesee hadn't experienced a more bizarre case in all the years he was involved with police work. All the statements and opinions he had gathered his first month of investigating all led to the same conclusion. There was no way Ron Beasley could have killed himself with a shotgun. He found no fault with that summation. What disturbed him was that no one bothered to investigate the unusual death and merely accepted point-blank what Sandra said, that Ron had killed himself.

Two weeks later, Keesee continued his probe. On December 9, he made a call to Anderson, South Carolina, to talk with a woman named Alpha Hennessee Chappell, who was a nurse's aide at Anderson Memorial Hospital. Back in the 1960s, she was a childhood sweetheart of Jerry Truesdale and also used to babysit for Sandra and Bill Fitch. When Jerry entered the army, their relationship abruptly ended.

Keesee was developing a pattern, one that associated Sandra with a gun. It was part of her character: cigarettes, black coffee and a gun.

Alpha verified it. "It was common knowledge that Sandra carried a pistol and would use it," she said.

She also corroborated what others had said, that Ron couldn't have killed himself. Alpha knew his condition well. He tried to talk but really couldn't and he seemed at times to know only his momma and daddy.

"One time Sandra walked by and Ron mumbled something that sounded like, 'she's a bad girl,' or something to that effect," added Alpha. "Her house became a very rough place to be in and I stopped going there."

It wasn't until a month after Christmas that Keesee became active once again on Sandra's case. On January 23, 1990, he received a telephone call from Coroner Joe Silvia in Winnsboro. He informed Keesee that Frances Truesdale came by his office that morning and requested a copy of the death report for Ron Beasley.

Keesee thanked him for the information. He realized now that Frances was aware that someone was investigating the years that she had been Sandra Beasley, particularly from March 1967 through July. But she didn't know who.

On the following day, James Rutland, Sandra and Ron's next-door neighbor, received a call from Keesee. In the early morning hours of the killing, he had left for an extended South Carolina National Guard training camp duty and didn't know anything about it until he returned home. He volunteered to Keesee that he knew Ron as well as anyone, before and after his stroke, and was certain he would have been unable to use a gun even if he held it in his hands.

The day before he left for guard duty, Rutland brought Ron a bowl of oyster stew. Since he was completely paralyzed on the right side and had very limited use of his left arm, Sandra had to feed him. "The stew ran down the side of his face and he could not even wipe it off," remarked Rutland.

Three months later, on April 26, 1990, Keesee appeared in Winnsboro again. In the Fairfield County Detention Center parking lot, he interviewed Mattie Caldwell, who worked for Sandra Beasley as an eighteen-year-old domestic after Ron suffered his stroke.

Betty Ruth McGinnis had picked up Mattie the morning of July 6, the fateful day that Ron was shot. She noticed there weren't any children in the house except eleven-month-old Jody. Nevertheless, she went about her chores. She began by cleaning Ron's bedroom as he sat in the living room. As soon as Mattie finished, Sandra made it a point to close the bedroom door.

It was the beginning of a pattern. After every room that Mattie cleaned, Sandra would shut the door. All the while, Mattie detected that Sandra was peeking at her from behind a newspaper, which made her feel uncomfortable. It wasn't just the heat, which became almost unbearable with all the doors being shut tight and no air conditioning, but Sandra was acting strange.

She instructed Mattie not to clean the kitchen but to go outside and take the clothes off the line and fold them there. Mattie had never done that before. She had always gathered the clothes in a basket and folded them inside the house, which now made her wonder what was going on. The television was louder than normal in the living room and the radio even louder in the kitchen.

Within minutes, Mattie heard a gunshot. She thought it came from somewhere down the road until Sandra appeared at the back door and motioned to Mattie to come into the house.

"Ron shot himself," said Sandra once they got inside. She then knelt down beside him for a moment, got up and ran for the telephone. Sandra was shaking so much she dropped the phone. Mattie picked it up.

"Who are you trying to call?" she asked.

"I was going to call Ron's mother, Mrs. Beasley."

Mattie made the call. Sandra then told her to hurry and clean up the blood on the living room floor. Mattie was surprised to find a towel on the floor near the gun rack. It hadn't been there when she had cleaned the room earlier, and she had no idea how it got there.

When the police arrived, Mattie heard Sandra describe what had happened. She said that Ron hopped to the back porch and got the bullets out of a box and then hopped back into the living room. Mattie thought this was odd. She never saw Ron move, and he always remained where he was put until someone moved him. He never once walked into the kitchen area or any place else in the house.

Sandra continued, much to Mattie's amazement. She told the police that Ron took a gun out of the rack, loaded it and shot at her as she ducked. Ron then stuck the gun in his mouth and killed himself. Mattie couldn't believe what she heard. She knew Ron was incapable of everything that Sandra described to the police. Mattie had placed the box of bullets on the shelf herself, and when she showed it to the police, the lid was still secure.

"On this particular morning, did you see Jerry Truesdale at the house?" inquired Keesee.

"Yes," answered Mattie quickly. "He came up the backyard and Sandra went out to the car to talk to him. He left, and she came back in the house."

"Was she having an affair with Jerry Truesdale during the time Ron was paralyzed?"

"Yes."

"And did she do a lot of partying?"

"Yes," Mattie answered for the third time.

"On Saturday, the day after the funeral, did you work at the house?"

Mattie indicated she dd. Only this time, she was accompanied by her sister, Delores.

"Why did you take Delores with you?" Keesee wanted to know.

"Because I was afraid of Sandra."

"Why were you afraid of her?"

"I was suspicious that she had killed Ron."

Keesee couldn't ask for more. He had a perfect witness in Mattie Caldwell. But he had more work to do. In assembling his reports, he felt he needed one more interview, with Ben Branham, which he felt would show Sandra's willingness to fire a gun. He contacted Investigator Fred Stewart Jr. of the Solicitor's Office for Fairfield County. Stewart agreed to conduct the interview and succeeded in scheduling it the morning of August 31, 1990, at the Fairfield County Courthouse.

Branham confirmed that Sandra pointed a gun at him while he was in bed with another woman in the bedroom of his house. "It was in the morning, and I brought a woman from Chester home since my wife and I were separated," said Branham. "We were in bed together, and all of a sudden my wife and Sandra Beasley and another woman broke the door down and ran into the bedroom. Sandra pointed a pistol in my direction."

"If you know what's good for you, it's best you lay right back down," she threatened. Ben wasn't about to take any chances. "Then my wife started beating up on me like a little girl. After they left, I called the police to ask them to watch my house after I left for work."

By now, Keesee was confident he had enough facts to present to the court that Frances Truesdale should be indicted for the murder of her husband, Jerry, after shooting him in the early morning hours of April 21, 1988. He could reveal that Frances, when she was known as Sandra Beasley some twenty years earlier, was no stranger to guns. She always carried one and knew how to use it and wouldn't hesitate if she had to.

And in the death of Jerry Truesdale, similar suspicions existed that occurred in Ron Beasley's demise in Winnsboro. Nobody talked about it in 1967, but amazingly they were doing so now.

Keesee realized that in his investigation of Frances Truesdale for the murder of her husband on April 23, 1988, he indeed found enough evidence to also indict her for the murder of Ron Beasley. But that was clearly something out of his jurisdiction, one that was the responsibility of Winnsboro authorities. His focus was strictly directed in obtaining a grand jury indictment in the slaying of Jerry Truesdale in Virginia, and he reserved whatever opinions he formulated about the Beasley killing until after that.

On November 5, 1990, a Roanoke grand jury indicted Frances T. Truesdale for murder. Keesee's two years of relentless investigation paid off. That was the first step. That same night, Frances was arrested on a forty-foot houseboat named *Serendipity* in a marina near Wilmington, North Carolina, living with her new boyfriend, Bob Citrano, an ex-convict she met shortly after Jerry Truesdale's funeral. Frances was doing all right for herself: a new boyfriend, a houseboat and a restaurant called the Smokehouse, before it closed. The insurance claims paid well, and whatever power she held over the men in her life, she energized well.

The best news the Virginia State Police received in a matter of seventy-two hours was that Frances wouldn't fight extradition. Instead, she was released on a $25,000 bond arranged by a local attorney after she spent the weekend in the New Hanover County Jail. Within forty-eight hours, she hired Anthony Anderson in Roanoke to handle her case there. Frances was the center of attention again. But this time, she didn't like it.

13

FRANCES TRUESDALE ON TRIAL

Appearing gaunt and conservatively dressed in a green suit, Frances Ann Truesdale walked up the steps of the Church Avenue courthouse in downtown Roanoke the morning of February 24, 1992, shortly before ten o'clock accompanied by her lawyer Anthony Anderson and two female legal associates. She was the Commonwealth of Virginia's Case No. CR90-1771, charged with the April 23, 1988 murder of her husband, Jerry Truesdale.

The trial was expected to last a week, and Frances couldn't believe that she was a defendant in a murder trial four years after her husband was killed. She thought she had gotten away with the heinous crime and was living on a houseboat with a new boyfriend in Winston-Salem. She appeared somber and without emotion like a business executive attending a meeting.

The Honorable Clifford R. Weckstein presided over the city's first murder case in twenty years. Weckstein was highly regarded in the legal arena and was looked up to as an extremely fair arbitrator. After the opening formalities were dispensed with and the clerk swore in Truesdale, who entered a plea of not guilty, Weckstein addressed his opening remarks to the defendant, looking directly at her. He informed Frances that before he could accept her not guilty plea, he had to ask her some questions; she could speak privately with her lawyers or ask him to explain the questions if she didn't understand them.

Frances stood erect and answered every question that Weckstein asked. She did not ask him to repeat a question and did not she excuse herself to consult with her attorneys. She was ready.

The lead attorney for her defense was Anthony Anderson of Roanoke, who was assisted by Melissa Friedman of his office. The third member of the team was Janet Pauca of Winston-Salem who appeared in legal jargon as pro hac vice, "for this turn or for this one particular occasion."

The Commonwealth's lead attorney was Donald Caldwell. His assistant was Betty Jo Anthony, the assistant Commonwealth attorney. They had to present a solid case of facts, most of which were circumstantial, that were culled after a yearlong investigation of a murder case that occurred four years earlier, if they hoped to influence a guilty verdict.

Continuing his pretrial decorum, Weckstein outlined the agenda for jury selection and then ordered the potential witnesses in the courtroom to leave and not discuss their pending testimony with anyone until the trial was over. The deputy sheriff escorted a number of witnesses out of Weckstein's court. Ann Letrick was not among them.

Both sides agreed on the system of admitting twenty-three jurors before the court. Each side was allowed to reject five jurors, leaving a total of thirteen who would judge the case, one being an alternate. The identity of the alternate would not be known until the jury retired and voted on a verdict. At that point in time, the alternate juror would be excused and not participate in deliberating the verdict.

Weckstein was pleased. He had recommended the jury system to both counselors, and they accepted. Weckstein greeted the jurors and identified himself as Cliff Weckstein, considerably less formal than Clifford. Weckstein was thorough. He spoke crisply and with authority, which had the attention of every juror. There wasn't even one yawn during his five-minute dissertation, and the defense was pleased with the manner in which he emphasized the defendant is presumed innocent.

After a brief recess, the jury returned to hear opening arguments. Caldwell got their attention first. He repeated the judge's contention that the defendant is innocent until proven guilty and that indeed the burden is on the Commonwealth to prove the case beyond a reasonable doubt. He assured the jurors that it wouldn't be a long, involved case, and some appeared relieved at that admission.

"In this type of case, especially where there are no confessions and no eyewitnesses to what happened, you will have to delve through the evidence that is available and determine whether or not Ms. Truesdale is guilty of the crime of murder," pointed out Caldwell.

"The evidence in this case will be that Mr. Truesdale, on the day he was shot, was taken to Roanoke Memorial and was put on life support. She represented that she had $25,000 worth of life insurance on Jerry Truesdale. Months later it was determined that she actually had about $285,000 of life insurance."

"What Mr. Caldwell has told you in his opening statement, and the court has advised you as well, Ms. Truesdale is innocent," began Anderson. "She is innocent of the crime for which she is charged. I anticipate that some of the evidence that you will hear, that on this night of hysteria when she was upset, when she was traumatized, that there will be statements that may be somewhat different than were made at a later date. You will hear those referred to as inconsistent statements, possibly, but I suggest to you at this juncture, please examine each one in careful detail."

Anderson, too, was carefully structuring his defense. He quickly made a point of circumstantial evidence and played upon trauma as a buffer for any inconsistencies that he knew existed in Frances's statements. Near the end of his monologue, he reverted to the circumstantial evidence theory.

"You have been told that the Commonwealth will rely on circumstantial evidence, and I, too, anticipate that this case will be largely about circumstantial evidence."

The first witness the prosecution summoned was Bill Conrad. It was no surprise. In a hearing in Judge Weckstein's chambers, Caldwell had requested that Conrad, a forensic expert, and Dr. David Oxley of the Chief Medical Examiner's Office be called as witnesses before the lunch break, stating the nature of their work required both to fulfill obligations that afternoon. Caldwell established Conrad's credentials strongly when he appeared before the court.

"If it is agreeable with Mr. Anderson, could we stipulate that he is an expert in his field?" asked Caldwell.

Anderson didn't hesitate anointing Conrad an expert. "Absolutely, Judge," agreed Anderson. "I know Mr. Conrad. I have had the benefit of being with him several times. I certainly stipulate his expertise."

Caldwell didn't waste any time. After Anderson's praise of Conrad, he quickly approached him with Exhibit One and asked the forensic expert to explain where it came from.

"The bullet was submitted by the Medical Examiner's Office," answered Conrad. "Dr. Oxley did the autopsy. What the bag contains is a mushroomed or damaged .22-caliber bullet."

The prosecuting attorney carefully walked Conrad through gun calibration for the benefit of the jury. He asked him to explain the difference between a .22 caliber and a .25 caliber.

"Three-thousandths of an inch," replied Conrad. Caldwell was positioning his line of questions.

"Is there any way this could be a .25-caliber bullet?"

"No, sir."

"Between a .22- and a .38-caliber bullet, is there a significant size difference there?"

"Yes, sir."

"In your opinion, could this bullet in any way have been a .38-caliber bullet?"

"No, sir."

Without any cross-examination, Caldwell then moved on to his next witness, Dr. Oxley. He identified himself to the court as the forensic pathologist and deputy chief medical examiner for Western Virginia. Before Oxley could answer Caldwell's question regarding his background and qualifications, Anderson interrupted.

"Judge, I am happy to stipulate Dr. Oxley's expertise in the field of forensic pathology as well," exclaimed Anderson.

Oxley revealed that several organs were removed from Truesdale's body—namely, the liver, kidney and spleen—at the request of Dr. C.E. Snecker, who asked permission for organ donations. However, Caldwell suffered somewhat of a setback when he couldn't get Oxley to say that he recognized the type of projectile or the size or caliber of the bullet that was lodged in Truesdale's brain. Anderson seemed pleased.

After a sixty-five-minute lunch break, Caldwell opened the afternoon session with a strong witness, Clarence Crouch. Frances didn't want him at the funeral and now he was here in court. She appeared a bit tense. Crouch had been working as a uniformed security guard for Mason Cove Security the night of the shooting and responded to her call for help on channel 19 of his CB radio. He was the first person to arrive at the van. He described what happened once he got there prepared to help.

"I asked her if I could check him for vital signs, but she wouldn't let me in the van," disclosed Crouch. "She was trying to tell me in her words what happened. She said, 'Well, I didn't mean to do this.' I see the gentleman lying in between the seats through the glass window. She repeated eight or twelve times, 'I didn't mean to do this.'"

"Is that lady that was in the van in the courtroom today?" asked Caldwell.

"Yes," replied Crouch.

"Can you point her out?"

"Yes," and Crouch pointed in the direction of Frances Truesdale.

Caldwell wanted to hammer home what Frances had said. It would make an impression on the jury members: "Now, what was the phrase that you testified that she repeated eight to twelve times?"

"I didn't mean to do this, eight to twelve times," repeated Crouch.

"What exactly did she say?"

"I didn't mean to do this."

No one in the courtroom could miss what Frances had repeatedly said that night. Caldwell made certain of that. He resumed questioning Crouch.

"Did you have occasion to attend the funeral of Jerry Truesdale?"

"Yes, I did."

"What was your purpose; how did you come to go there?"

"I was called by one of her sons. I don't know what his name was. He called and left a message with my mother; would I like to attend his father's funeral. So, in my respect, I did."

That wasn't what Frances wanted to hear. Not at all. She took offense when Crouch appeared at the funeral home, making a point to ask what he was doing here and who asked him to come. She was upset by his presence.

In his cross-examination, Anderson wanted Crouch to re-create the scene the night he first came in contact with the van and talked to Frances.

"Was she crying?"

"Not at first, but when the first aid and the police department got there, she did."

"Did she have blood on her when you arrived?"

"Evidently, because I was trying to comfort her, and she got against me and it got off from her onto my shirt."

The first Roanoke police officer to arrive on the scene was Lieutenant C.D. Allen. Back in 1988, he was a sergeant, and his initial contact with Frances was significant. He found her being consoled by Crouch.

"I was trying to find out exactly what was going on, and she was hysterical and screaming and yelling, and it took me about twenty or thirty seconds before she finally informed me that her husband had been shot and [was] lying in the back of the van," Allen told the court.

"I looked inside and found a white male, later identified as Jerry Truesdale, lying on either clothing or a blanket, some type of what I would call a pallet, lying on his back with his feet up into the passenger's side chair. I tried to learn from the female exactly what happened, and it became very confusing, as she would tell me one thing, and when I would try to get her to pinpoint it, she would tell me another thing. I knew that we were going to have a jurisdiction problem, so I called the Roanoke County Sheriff's Department. While I was waiting for them to show up, she started talking again, and finally she had changed it so many times that I just told our dispatcher to get the state police and have them send an investigator. That is when they dispatched Trooper Keesee."

Caldwell turned to Allen for his next question, standing just to the left of him, not allowing himself to come between the witness and the jury. As Allen was the first law officer at the crime scene, his testimony was relevant, and the attorney wanted to make certain the jurors heard in every detail. And like Anderson, he was waiting to dramatize a point.

"When she told you that her husband had gotten out of the van, did you have her describe what happened?"

"She stated that at first he had gotten out of the van and had taken only a couple of steps when she heard the gunshot, and that he fell back into the driver's seat of the van, and that she lifted him from the ground and put him into the back part. She slid from the passenger's side to the driver's side and picked him up and moved him into the back cargo of the van. I didn't understand exactly what she was talking about. So, I had Officer Martin, who was there at the scene, sit on the passenger's side. Then I positioned Ms. Truesdale up and back until she could tell me yes, this was where her husband was when she heard the gunshot."

J.C. Martin, a female officer from the Roanoke City Police Department, followed Allen on the stand. She arrived at the scene of the shooting just minutes after Allen got there and corroborated what he said earlier, only more graphically.

"When I was beside the victim, he was already gurgling," began Martin. "He was either choking on his own blood or he was having a difficult time breathing. It seemed to me that it was a possibility that we were going to lose this man."

"What, if anything, did Ms. Truesdale say in your presence?" asked Caldwell. In reply, Martin explained what she heard Frances tell Allen, that there were two males, she couldn't tell if they were white or Black, who fled in a black Granada with what appeared to be a New York license plate that began with the letters RUD.

Frances maintained her story, which was consistent, that she and her husband had left a rest area and headed south on Highway 81. He was driving at the time, but they had been taking turns because they were on their way to North Carolina. At the time he was driving, another vehicle came up close behind and started blinking its lights. Frances claimed her husband became upset, so much so that he pulled over to the side of the road to see what was wrong.

She said that her husband stepped from the vehicle when she heard a gunshot. She then climbed across the seat of the van and pulled him back in.

"About that time, I felt a little bit uncertain about what she had said," remarked Martin.

Anderson leaped to his feet with an objection. "Your Honor, 'uncertain about,' that is a conclusion on her part."

Weckstein overruled the challenge and instructed the prosecution to go ahead.

"Explain what you mean by uncertain?" asked Caldwell.

Martin replied, "When she described herself pulling him back into the vehicle, after seeing his body and looking at her, I felt it seemed almost as if it were impossible for her to."

Caldwell cut her off. She was moving into an area of judgment, and he wanted to avoid that. "Don't get into that. Don't express a conclusion, but that is what she said she had done?"

"She said she had done that. So, I asked her again where was her husband standing when this happened? At the time she said that he had only turned his seat and was getting out of the vehicle when he was shot, and she was still in the passenger's seat and she just pulled him back across. Sergeant Allen and I were not quite certain of what she was explaining, and we tried to do a little experiment with her and show us what occurred. The first time she showed her husband moving completely out of the van. The second time she did it, she showed him just like turning and moving one leg out of the van, not getting all the way out. When the rescue vehicle was ready to leave, [I] asked if there was anything she wanted out of the van. She said she needed her purse. [I said] 'I'll go back and get that for you.' 'No, I will get it myself,' she said. Almost at a run, she came back to the van with me. I reached in and picked up the purse and she grabbed it from me. She just grabbed it."

Caldwell wanted to establish one more point. And he did. He got Martin to concur that Frances got angry with Allen. "She told him to go out and find the people that done this and quit asking questions," disclosed Martin. "At one point she got very angry with Sergeant Allen."

Caldwell was doing fine. And he hadn't even gotten to Ann Letrick.

No one in Winnsboro or the city of Roanoke or Barry Keesee, for that matter, knew that Ann Letrick was in the Roanoke courthouse the morning of February 24, 1992. And nobody inside the courtroom except Caldwell and his staff knew that she was there. Jerry Truesdale's baby sister was sequestered in Caldwell's office away from everybody. She was a key witness, and he wanted to protect her.

Ann felt some apprehension as she waited to testify. Her appearance as the final witness of the day would identify her as the one who initiated the investigation three years ago and why Frances Truesdale was sitting in the courtroom as a defendant. It was not a pleasant thought, and Ann knew she would be scorned by everyone in Frances's family and looked on as someone who betrayed them. But it was her brother who was killed by Frances' evil hand, and she wasn't going to let her get away with it.

And she sat there isolated in a strange office two hundred miles from home thinking about the older woman, one her brother deeply loved, one she always called Sandra, never Frances. He was totally devoted to her, gave her anything she wanted in the twenty-one years they had been married, really without any signs of unhappiness. He helped raise her four young boys, who called him daddy before his own son, Jerry, was born.

They had done so much and went so far together. Just two months before his death he was looking forward to retiring in June and operating a gas station that both of them had already leased in Winston-Salem. After driving the roads for fifteen years in a Pilot truck, Jerry was content to being home nights, a retired truck driver at the age of forty-one.

Ann thought about how Jerry was always there for her. They had a close relationship, more so than anyone else in the family. Once, when she was small and needed stitches, it was Jerry holding her hand in the doctor's office. When Ann's first son was born, it was Jerry comforting her in the hospital. He was like a second father to her.

"If something ever happens to Momma, don't you let anybody else call me. You call me," he ordered.

Ann might have been the youngest in the family of eight, but she was very special to Jerry. Even after she got married and had two sons of her own, they remained close.

Memories. Only memories. That's all she had left. Whatever she said or did would never erase them, and she knew she had to testify. She knew that the day she started the investigation with a phone call to the Virginia State Police. She had all those years to get ready. That time was now.

And she was ready to walk into the courtroom, face Frances, and tell what she knew.

When Betty Jo, Caldwell's assistant, summoned her as the last witness of the day, she took a deep breath and walked down the corridor alongside her to the courtroom. She walked in confidently, remembering what Caldwell had told her the last time they talked that morning.

"Always look at the jury," he impressed upon her. "Always look at the jury," she reminded herself as she entered the courtroom, knowing that Frances would be shocked at seeing her.

She glanced at Frances as she walked to take the stand. She had to, only to break the tension. Frances slumped into her chair and turned and looked at her attorney. At that very moment, she knew it was Ann who fingered her. Frances didn't want to look at her. As soon as she took the oath, she sat with her body in the direction of the jury to make certain she would be looking at them when she answered Caldwell's very first question. He asked her to describe the hospital scene when she first saw Frances.

"When you went to the hospital, would you tell the members of the jury what you did?"

Ann, a little excited at first, began to relax and related to the jury her conversation with Frances. It began with the fact that Jerry had been shot by two guys driving a black car with a New Jersey license plate. However, when her mother and the rest of the members of the family joined them, Frances repeated her tale about the black car, only this time she said it had a New York plate that started with the letters RUD.

Frances repeated the details of what had happened before the shooting, the same story she had told to the police. She was convincing. One juror, who appeared skeptical, wiped a tear from his eye. Ann wasn't nervous anymore.

"Then she started on different stuff," continued Ann. "She was really upset because she said if Jerry died, they only had a $25,000 life insurance policy and she didn't know how she was going to pay the bills. She said they had ordered three wreckers because he was going to retire in June, and they were on their way back to Winston-Salem to pick them up. She tried to tell Jerry not to order those wreckers because they could wait but Jerry said since he was retiring in June, they could use them at the gas station they owned. She was real upset, and she went out to the stairway to smoke, and I went with her and she said that he had been shot with a .22-caliber handgun. I knew that Sandra owned a .22-caliber handgun because she had showed it to me one time at my home. She told me that was the size I needed because you can carry it with you at all times. That started my suspicions. She told Mr. Keesee about having a .38-caliber handgun. Sandra told me in the wintertime she carried the .22 caliber in her boot for protection and in the summer in her makeup bag. Several different times at Momma's she would have to run in the house and get her purse because of the grandkids and she wouldn't want one of them to shoot themselves."

In his cross-examination, Anderson couldn't shake Ann or uncover any flaws in her testimony. Frances Truesdale could hold nothing but hate for her. Ann Truesdale walked out of that courtroom a confident woman.

Left: Ron "Little Red" Beasley.

Right: Mattie Caldwell, Beasley's neighbor and baby sitter.

Sheriff Herman Young. *Courtesy of Fairfield County.*

Attorney Creighton Coleman. *Courtesy of Janice Haynes.*

Top: Defense Attorney
Bob Fitzsimmons.
*Courtesy of Regina Bagley
Anderson.*

Bottom: Fairfield County
Courthouse, Architect
Robert Mills. *Courtesy of
Jim Schmid.*

Sheriff's Office. *Courtesy of Emma Vess.*

Left: Historical Marker, Fairfield County Courthouse. *Courtesy of Emma Vess.*

Below: Winnsboro Post Office. *Courtesy of Emma Vess.*

Winnsboro Town Hall. *Courtesy of Emma Vess.*

Town Sign. *Courtesy of Emma Vess.*

Grave site of Ronald Beasley. *Courtesy of Emma Vess.*

Winnsboro's busiest intersection.

You are cordially invited to attend a Reception hosted by
Senator Creighton Coleman and Representative MaryGail Douglas
and
The Fairfield Intergovernmental Coalition

Honoring

Sheriff Herman Young, Retired

and

Confirmed Recipient of The Order of the Palmetto
by
Governor Nikki R. Haley
on
Monday, the 23rd of February, Two Thousand and fifteen
From five thirty until eight pm in the evening
at
The Carolina Event Center
1122 US Highway 321, Winnsboro, South Carolina

Presentation of the Award at 6:30 pm by Mr. Leroy Smith,
Director, South Carolina Department of Public Safety

Please RSVP by the 18th day of February to the Fairfield Chamber
of Commerce at 803-635-4242 or email to fchamber@truvista.net

Years of Serivce 1992-2014

Sheriff Herman Young was awarded The Order of the Palmetto.

HENRY MCMASTER
ATTORNEY GENERAL

April 23, 2009

Sheriff Herman Young
Fairfield Sheriff's Office
P. O. Box 387
Winnsboro, SC 29180

   Re: Frances S. Truesdale
     SCDC# 222145

Dear Sheriff Young:

We are pleased to advise you that Frances S. Truesdale was denied his request for appeal in the Federal District Court.

As a reminder, the possibility of Frances S. Truesdale filing an appeal to the Fourth Circuit Court of Appeals remains. Our Office attempts to make every reasonable effort to contact you and advise of case decisions. Again, let me stress that these requests for a new trial are rarely granted by the court. Also, these actions may take years to complete. The inmate should remain in custody throughout this process barring sentence completion or the offender being granted parole.

Please remember to keep your address and telephone numbers current with the South Carolina Department of Corrections as well as our Agency. You may reach the Department of Corrections toll-free at 1-800-835-0304 to advise of any corrections. If you have any questions or concerns, please call this Office toll-free at 1-800-213-5652.

Sincerely,

Marie Higgins

Marie Higgins
Victim Services Specialist
MH/mh

REMBERT C. DENNIS BUILDING • POST OFFICE BOX 11549 • COLUMBIA, SC 29211-1549 • TELEPHONE 803-734-3970 • FACSIMILE 803-253-6283

The request for parole is denied.

SC Department of Probation, Parole and Pardon Services
Pre-Parole Notification

To: Sheriff Herman Young
    PO Box 387
    Winnsboro, SC 29180

Date: January 11, 2006

From: John Hutto
      PO Box 60
      Winnsboro, SC 29180
Phone #: (803) 635-5466

Inmate: Frances Truesdale, AKA: Sandra Beasley
Projected Hearing Date: March 1, 2006
SCDC #: 222145
Offense: Murder
Indictment: 96-GS-20-29
Date of Sentence: November 20, 1996

The above named offender has a projected parole hearing date, as indicated above. This office is presently conducting a pre-parole investigation which will be used by the Parole Board in making a decision to grant or deny parole. Your cooperation in providing relevant information in this matter as well as your recommendation for or against parole is greatly appreciated.

Once an exact date has been scheduled, you will be notified by the Office for Victim Services prior to that date and given the opportunity to appear before the Parole Board or to submit a written statement to review, provided that this specific sentence has not been satisfied.

Please answer the questions listed below and return this form within five (5) working days to the address at the top of this form.

Please circle one response:
1). I am opposed to parole.   2). I am neutral in regards to parole.   3). I am in favor of parole.

Comments:

Signature: _Herman W. Young_   Date: _Jan 25, 06_

Federal Court appeal is denied.

14

KEESEE THE KEY WITNESS

On the second day of the trial, there was a noticeable increase in the number of spectators seated in the Roanoke County Courthouse. The courtroom was half empty on Monday, but media coverage of the day-old trial stimulated interest throughout the city of Roanoke. Murder trials weren't common in the city, and one of a death that had occurred four years earlier certainly added to the intrigue. Was the accused a loving wife devoted to her children or a cold bloodied killer? It was the stuff of movies with its onerous overtones.

The scheduled appearance of Barry Keesee on the witness stand played out the drama. Frances Truesdale's tormentor for the past two years would have the stage for the morning session all to himself, and she would lay her eyes on him for the first time in four years. His testimony was expected to be lengthy, and the attorney for the Commonwealth, Don Caldwell, wanted him to appear first. Caldwell took into consideration that in the morning hours the jury would be fresh and wouldn't tire as easily if Keesee took up the entire morning on the witness stand.

Keesee was sedulous in assembling a case against Frances. Although the case he brought before the courts was circumstantial in nature, he exuded confidence that his two years in the field would result in a conviction. The veteran investigator had been involved in dozens of cases, but none intrigued him more than this one and he was prepared to show why to a jury of twelve in a crowded courtroom.

Caldwell made a peculiar point in the beginning of his interrogation. He asked Keesee why he didn't wear a uniform on the night he was called to the crime scene. When Keesee answered that he didn't have one, Caldwell pressed him to explain that to the jury because they had never seen him before, and they didn't understand that.

Before Keesee could elucidate, Tony Anderson raised an objection, explaining to Judge Clifford Weckstein that he didn't understand the relevance of the question. He was overruled.

"I am assigned as a plainclothes investigator and I haven't been in uniform since 1970," explained Keesee.

With that statement, Caldwell then asked Keesee to describe what took place at the crime scene when he arrived. Caldwell expected a detailed description. The victim can be murdered only once, but the scene can be murdered one hundred times. Keesee began his testimony.

"Sergeant C.D. Allen of the Roanoke City Police Department was the ranking member at the crime scene. After I got in touch with him, I started my investigation at his request. My investigation lasted for several minutes at the van. Right behind the driver's seat there was a pallet, and on this pallet, I observed bloody clothing. There was a bloody T-shirt, a bloody long-sleeve plaid shirt, a bloody pillow, a bloody blanket and underneath the blanket was a white mattress cover.

"I then took my flashlight, and I looked in the interior and exterior of the van for any bullet holes or any other noticeable damage and I didn't see any. I also looked to see if there was blood anywhere else in the van, inside or outside, other than on the pallet area. I didn't see any blood anywhere, except on the pallet area. I asked Sergeant Allen if he would take precautions in having the van towed or driven to the Roanoke City Garage, which is the area that Roanoke City stores vehicles for safekeeping. He assured me he would.

"I was still in a state of confusion as to what actually was going on. I needed to talk to an eyewitness as soon as possible. So, I went to the Roanoke Memorial Hospital emergency room. I arrived there at approximately 6:30 a.m. on Thursday, April 21, 1988. I went into the emergency room area and saw a man lying on a stretcher. Through my experience in homicide investigations, it was obvious he was hooked to life support equipment.

"As the doctor was working on him, I observed what appeared to be a small bullet wound right behind his left ear. It appeared he was in pretty critical shape and the doctors and the staff that was working on him thought so, too. I stayed for a few minutes longer and then left and made my way down to the nurses' station. One of the nurses directed me to a small room and introduced me to a lady as Ms. Truesdale."

Keesee was thorough and in total command of his delivery as the jury listened intently. He was precise in his detail of the crime scene, making a point of the mattress cover being white, which really didn't have any relevancy to the murder itself. Keesee was demonstrating to the jury that he was in command of everything that went on that night, and Caldwell was pleased. That is what he intended Keesee to do and why he wanted him in the box first. Keesee continued without interruption, and he had the jury's attention.

"She said her maiden name was Frances Ann Scott and she had been married to Mr. Truesdale for approximately twenty years. She told me she had six children, five boys and a girl. During the time I was in the room, I talked to some of her children and to a friend of hers, a neighbor by the name of Gene Deal.

"I asked her if anybody else was with them when her husband was shot, and she said that nobody was present, that she was the only one in the van with him. Ms. Truesdale told me that her husband was a truck driver for Pilot Freight Lines and that he had been driving out of the branch office at Camp Hill, Pennsylvania, for the last several months, a year or so.

"She told me that they traveled from Camp Hill to a rest area just outside of Roanoke on Interstate 81 South. She was driving and her husband was asleep on the pallet behind the driver's seat. They had to use the restroom, so she pulled into the rest area just before you get to Roanoke, in the southbound lane of I-81.

"After using the facilities, she came out at the same time her husband did. She noticed two young white males walking behind her husband saying something. She asked Jerry what they wanted, and he is supposed to have told her that, 'They ain't nothing but a couple of damn bums. They wanted change for a $20. I was going to give them two $10s, but they don't even have a $20,' she said Mr. Truesdale told her.

"She said both of them were real neat looking, young men, short military hair, no facial hair. She described one being shorter than the other and both had dark hair. The shorter man grabbed Jerry's arm and said, 'We need some money. Come on man, give us some money. I will let you hold my watch.'

"He talked with a northern accent, as if he was from New York City. When he grabbed Mr. Truesdale's arm, Mr. Truesdale swung around and backhanded him in the mouth and that she heard Mr. Truesdale's ring hit the young man's teeth. She got in to drive the van and Jerry pulled her out of the way saying that he was going to drive.

"As they were leaving the parking lot, Mr. Truesdale made a statement to her, 'There goes those two damn bums. They are getting into that New York Ford.' She said she noticed that the letters on the tag, the first three letters, were RUD."

Keesee was doing exactly what Caldwell expected. He was weaving his story effectively, without supposition or opinion that could have created an objection from the defense. There wasn't any, and Caldwell realized he had the perfect witness in Keesee. He was the most important one that the Commonwealth had in presenting circumstantial evidence and a verdict of guilty. Keesee went on, and his next recital caught the attention of several jurors.

"Ms. Truesdale told me as they got back onto Interstate 81, she and Mr. Truesdale became very argumentative with each other about him striking the young man in the mouth. She was cursing at him, and he was cursing at her.

"She said they had traveled a long distance down 81 South when all of a sudden this same black Ford Granada passed the van and immediately cut back in front, into the right lane. She knew it was the same Ford Granada because she was sitting in the captain's chair on the passenger's side and was looking at the license tag and she saw the letters again, RUD.

"Then the driver of that vehicle hit his brakes and Mr. Truesdale hit the brakes on the van and then immediately pulled out to the left and passed the Ford Granada. She said that the black Ford Granada came right behind the van and threw the high beams right into the back window of the van.

"Her husband started to stop and slammed on his brakes and said, 'I guess I will have to whip the mother fucker's ass now.' 'I begged him not to get out of the van. I was sitting on the passenger's chair telling him to please not get out.' He opened the door, and just as he cracked it, she saw the face of the young man that he had struck in the mouth.

"She had a pillow that she was holding in her arm, and she usually held a pillow because she used to be a thumb sucker. When she saw the young man's face, she saw a gun in his hand and the gun was right behind her husband's head. She then lunged forward with the pillow and the gun went off.

"'I touched his arm,' she told me. 'I touched his arm as it fired. The sound was deafening. I heard the other man outside of the van somewhere, but I didn't see him, holler out, 'You crazy mother fucker.' 'My husband was still under the wheel and I jumped under the wheel and spun off while throwing him into the back of the van. I noticed I was going away from the city, away from the lights. I was going away from where I figured a hospital would be.'

"I asked her what kind of gun was it that the man shot her husband with? She said, 'I don't know. I don't know anything about guns. I have never owned a gun. I am afraid of guns. My husband just recently bought a little gun about two weeks ago. It is in our luggage inside of the van in a carrying case. It is silver.'"

Caldwell strategically stopped Keesee's monologue at that juncture. He did so dramatically to establish that Frances was lying about guns. Most of the witnesses had verified that Frances always had a gun in her possession and that she knew how to fire one. Somehow, the defense remained quiet as Caldwell took Keesee back to the emergency room at the hospital to establish for the benefit of the jury a motive for the murder. Keesee's memory remained clear.

"Ms. Truesdale was sitting there and looking down into the area where her husband was lying. You couldn't see where he was from where we were at in this little waiting room. But she looked down towards the area where he was and said, 'Jerry Truesdale, you left us in a heck of a mess.'

"I asked her what she was talking about. She said, 'He left us with all kinds of bills. He left us in debt. We are, were, in the process of buying the building that we run a service station at, Cardinal Union 77 Service Station in Winston-Salem, North Carolina. He had just ordered three new wreckers, two trucks. I told him not to do it, but, no, he wouldn't listen. He is hardheaded. The two trucks have already been built and we have to pick them up in a couple of days.'

"Sensing her frustrations, I tried to relieve some of her anxiety by telling her, 'Well, if he doesn't make it, maybe his insurance will tide you and your boys over until things can be worked out.' She said, 'That won't do much. That won't even cover the building on the wrecker place, or the service station that we are buying.'

"'Well, how much insurance does Mr. Truesdale have on his life?' She said, 'He ain't got but $25,000 and that is through the Teamsters Union. We can use that to bury him and then give the boys a little bit of that, and there ain't much of that left.'"

Keesee continued his testimony, and no one in the courtroom appeared bored. He told of how he went back to the hospital the next day and asked Truesdale if she needed anything else. She told him that she was waiting for relatives and friends to arrive from North and South Carolina, revealing that when she lived there, they knew her by a nickname, Sandra.

Keesee had more work to do. He asked Ms. Truesdale if she would accompany him on a trip to the highway and try to find exactly where her husband had been shot. She asked if her neighbor, Deal, could go with them along with one of her sons, and they sat in the back seat while Frances occupied the passenger seat up front so she could better describe where the crime had taken place. Keesee recorded on his odometer a distance of twenty-four and a half miles from the rest area to the crime scene.

Judge Weckstein spoke out at that point: "Sometime in the next ten to fifteen minutes, the jury probably would appreciate a recess."

Caldwell agreed. "If you want to break now, that would be fine."

"There is some appreciation of that idea," smiled Weckstein.

"Ladies and gentlemen, we will take a ten- or fifteen-minute recess."

Feeling refreshed, Keesee sat tall in the witness stand. He said that when they returned to the hospital from the crime scene later that afternoon, Frances asked him about the van.

"I want you to clean the bloody clothes out, the bloody items, because I don't want my son or my children to see the blood in the van," she told Keesee. It was still daylight when Keesee arrived at the Roanoke City garage. He decided to check the van a second time.

"I didn't find any holes in the van. I didn't find any blood inside the van, on the seats, on the steering wheel or on the dash or on the console in between. I only found blood in the van back on the pallet area. I took the pillow that was laying on the pallet that was soaked in blood and the T-shirt and long-sleeve plaid shirt that had obviously been cut off of Mr. Truesdale before being transported to the hospital.

"They were laying on a blanket that also had blood on it. I took these items, and I put them in a white plastic bag and placed them in my police car. I also took the white mattress cover laying on the floorboard right behind the driver's seat. I folded it up and I laid it back in the back part of the van. I didn't take that. I have retained those since then."

Caldwell then turned his attention to the getaway car. He wanted to impress on the jury how extensively Keesee searched for it and never found it. He was establishing the fact that such an automobile never existed. Keesee's answers were short and snappy.

"Were you ever able to find a black Ford Granada with this partial tag on it that led anywhere?"

"No."

"What about the two suspects?"

"Nothing."

Keesee answered that the search for the vehicle continued through the assistance of the New York State Police until July 1989. He disclosed that there were just five Ford Granadas in the state in April 1988 that had tags beginning with RUD. None of them was black.

"Did there ever come a point in time when you received other information that led you to open up a second part of your investigation?" asked Caldwell.

"Yes. Approximately three weeks after Mr. Truesdale was murdered, I had contact with Lieutenant Don Shields with the Roanoke City Police Department, Criminal Investigation Division. He put me in contact with a woman in Winnsboro, South Carolina, named Ann Letrick. I contacted her on May 20, 1988."

"Were you contacted by any other sources that made you begin to concentrate in other areas?"

"I was contacted by insurance companies, and I learned that there was substantial amounts of insurance, hundreds of thousands of dollars more insurance on the life of Mr. Truesdale than that which Ms. Truesdale had told me the morning of Thursday, April 21, 1988."

Caldwell had no more questions. He didn't need any. He succeeded in getting Keesee to lay out a perfect plot leading to the wanton murder of Jerry Truesdale. Keesee was effectively brilliant in his narration, and Caldwell felt good about what the jury heard in Keesee's two hours on the stand.

"Mr. Anderson, if you want to cross-examine now, depending how long it is?" asked Judge Weckstein.

"Judge, I would like to suggest to the court that maybe this is an appropriate time to break for the lunch hour," said Anderson. "I anticipation cross-examination may be longer than just a few minutes," added Anderson, setting the stage for the afternoon session.

There was no doubt that Keesee left a poignant impression on the jury. He definitely fulfilled the perception of a special investigator, lucid, confident and knowledgeable. Anderson had to puncture holes in his testimony, and he knew he faced a difficult task. He had the entire lunch hour to think about it. His first pertinent question was regarding Keesee's first contact with his client in the hospital.

"That is when you began to question her of what her knowledge was of the events that had happened that had led you there?" asked Anderson.

Keesee didn't give him a simple yes. Instead, he outlined a more detailed answer: "That is when the process of introducing myself and the inquiry began. It didn't happen in a sequence of events of going right into everything right there because she was telling me about her children in Winston-Salem, that some had been called, and that she needed to call some others. It was very, very confusing as far as her children go as far as I am concerned because I didn't know her, didn't know her family situation."

The word *confusing* jumped at Anderson. He came back quickly with his next question and phrased it flawlessly: "After you kind of got through the first stage of the confusion, and understandably because you had a traumatic experience on your hands that day, you began to reach a point where you wanted to talk with Ms. Truesdale about what had happened?"

Keesee responded affirmatively.

"And it was at that time that Ms. Truesdale began to cooperate with you regarding this investigation, isn't that true?"

"She cooperated when it was to her benefit."

Anderson scowled. He didn't like the response. He spoke with an angry correction, fully addressing Keesee by name. "That is not my question, Special Agent Keesee. My question is, isn't it true that she began to cooperate with you at that time?"

Anderson got the yes he was seeking. He pursued further. "Is it fair to say that at this time Ms. Truesdale was upset and concerned about the condition of her husband?"

Keesee didn't budge.

"She never did appear upset to me. She only appeared tired."

"She only appeared tired. You never saw her cry?" Keesee remained firm.

"She never cried with me."

Anderson couldn't establish with Keesee that Frances was traumatized from the moment she sat in the hospital in the Intensive Care Unit until she began relating to him the facts that occurred earlier that night. That would have accounted for the inconsistencies in what she had told others. Anderson tried to make it appear that it was Keesee who was inconsistent. Keesee remained rigid and focused.

"Did she tell you that the shooting took place after she came out of the highway construction site, not before where the construction had started? That is not what she told you that morning at the hospital?"

He got a no: "She said after her husband was shot, she went through a construction area."

Anderson continued this line of questioning. He was determined to uncover a flaw in Keesee's description, which would be a major accomplishment in his defense.

"She later described to you the point of where this incident happened was through that construction site in the curve that you have identified in the pictures, isn't that true?"

"No, sir. When she told me in the hospital that after her husband was shot that she passed through a construction area, based on what I had found in my investigation of where the van was located on Hershberger Road, it was my understanding that he was shot at the intersection of 1-581 and 81 South. She had passed through this construction area after he was shot."

"So, when I asked you earlier was it that report that you were able to draw your conclusion from that morning, you answered me, yes. Are you saying now that that is not correct?"

Keesee was unruffled by the challenge. He leaned forward in his chair to make his point.

"I am saying the facts of the situation is that my conclusions were drawn from the statements she made at the hospital, based on my investigation that I had conducted at Hershberger Road where the van was located, that her husband was shot at the intersection of 581 and 81 South. After she told me that she traveled through a construction area after her husband was shot, I concluded she had traveled from I-581, 81 South intersection where he was shot, through the construction area down on 581 South."

Keesee sat back, waiting for the next question. Anderson walked around and then looked at him.

"I am a little bit confused. The incident that she told you about took place after she came out of the construction on South 581?"

"That was what she showed me."

"No, sir. That is what she told you. Isn't that true?"

"When she was showing me, she was telling me."

Anderson had more than he bargained for. Keesee was a relentless witness, unnerved. Anderson couldn't puncture any of his answers. He went in another direction with his questioning. He made a point that Keesee had several conversations with Ms. Truesdale.

"She would either call or I would call her, and she would inquire if I had developed any suspects into who was responsible for killing her husband."

Anderson was attempting to show that Ms. Truesdale was concerned about the killers and that she would help in any way through her phone calls. Anderson went on.

"Special Agent Keesee, did there come a time when you traveled to Winston-Salem, North Carolina, to meet with Ms. Truesdale?"

"I met with her at her residence on September 13, 1989."

"Did you take a statement from her at that time?"

"At this time, I took a recorded statement from her, yes, sir."

"And in that recorded statement, she again went through with you what she had previously told you, didn't she, Special Agent Keesee?"

"She didn't tell me everything the same way she told me the first time."

Anderson had no more questions. He didn't succeed sullying Keesee's testimony.

In his redirect, Caldwell cleverly outlined his approach. He concentrated on the crime scene only, specifically at the time that Jerry Truesdale was shot. He referred to the taped statement that Keesee got from Ms. Truesdale on September 13, 1989, and the part where she said that "he opened the door." What was her next response?

"'He opened the door. I literally…' At that point I interrupted her, 'I thought you.' Ms. Truesdale said, 'No, he opened it. His foot was out the door. His foot was out the door and I pulled off. I was holding onto his arm and screaming and cussing. You can't act like this, I remember saying. All they got to do is hit you.'"

"So, basically, when she gave you her statement, when her husband was shot, the door was open, and his foot was out the door?"

"On this occasion she said his foot was outside of the door."

"Is that what she told you that morning on April 21?"

"No. She said that he had just opened the door. He was still under the wheel when she saw the young man who killed him or had the gun. She lunged towards him and touched his arm and touched the gun. She jumped under the wheel and took control of the vehicle, all the time, while she was under the wheel trying to throw him and throwing him into the back part of the van. On this occasion his foot was out of the van and she was dragging, and she was holding his arm and screaming and cussing as she drove off."

Keesee finally stepped down. He walked tall, feeling good about himself. He delivered his testimony mellifluously. Frances Truesdale never wanted to see him again.

15

CONDUCT AND MOTIVE

There was no doubt that Keesee was an impressive witness for the prosecution. A number of spectators whispered to one another as he walked out of the courtroom. Anderson turned to his client, Frances Truesdale, with a forlorn look but maintained his decorum. Keesee was impervious, which made Anderson's defense that much more difficult. In a game of chess that is courtroom trial, he was losing.

Caldwell moved through his next three witnesses easily and quickly. He got Barbara Martin, a registered nurse who was a nurse's aide when Frances was hospitalized in 1965, to tell the court that as Sandra Fitch she had a gun in her possession.

"I have it for my protection," Frances told her. Martin, who was only sixteen at the time, became frightened. She reported the presence of a gun to the head nurse who quickly removed it from Frances's possession and locked the gun in a safe. Before Martin could describe how big Fairfield Memorial Hospital in Winnsboro was, Anderson objected.

"I want to object to the relevance of that," remarked Anderson. "This may be a good time for a brief recess."

Weckstein saw through the objection. "Is there a matter you think needs to be taken up?" he inquired.

When Anderson said that he did, Weckstein asked the jury to leave the courtroom. Anderson then approached the bench.

"Judge, I want to interpose an objection at this juncture to the relevancy of this line of questioning, as well as to the remoteness of it at the time. This happened in 1965. We have not heard any evidence, and maybe that is what he is going into, to see if it is in any way connected to the present time or to April of 1988." Weckstein asked Caldwell to comment.

"The testimony from Agent Keesee that is before the court is that when she was questioned about the gun, she said she didn't own one, didn't know anything about a gun and she was scared of guns. The Commonwealth not only intends to offer this witness, but two others to show that at least as early as 1965 through at least 1987 that it was on three different occasions, she carried a gun in her pocketbook."

Weckstein gave his ruling. He sustained Anderson's objection to the size of the hospital. But he overruled Anderson's concern about the relevancy of gun possession. When Anderson didn't have anything more to argue about the subject, the jury was called back into the courtroom.

Caldwell asked Betty Ruth McGinnis to take the stand. She told the court that she knew Frances Truesdale as Sandra Beasley in the sixties. She also confirmed that she lived with her for a period of four months to help her with the children. When Caldwell posed the next question about, to her knowledge, if Sandra owned any type of weapons, Anderson raised an objection that was denied.

"I knew that she routinely carried a handgun in her pocketbook," declared Betty Ruth.

William Cooper of Winston-Salem was the prosecution's third witness of the afternoon. He would turn out to be the last one summoned by the Commonwealth. Caldwell took his witness back to 1987 and a conversation he had with Frances Truesdale at the service station she operated in Winston-Salem.

"I was in the service station, and we were talking," related Cooper. "I don't know how we brought it up about guns and Frances showed me a little gun. I said, 'Frances, let me have that little gun. I got one and I will trade with you.' She said, 'No, I ain't going to trade. I ain't going to get rid of my gun'.

"I was kidding with her and never thought that much about it. I went back to my truck and got my gun and showed it to her because I was trying to trade with her, and she said no."

"Where was she keeping the gun that she showed you?" asked Caldwell.

"It was in her pocketbook."

Anderson took another approach to the gun question hanging over his client's head. He attempted to create doubt in his crossexamination with his first question to Cooper.

"Did you know that Jerry Truesdale had purchased a gun for Frances and given it to her?" He got a no. He also got the same reply when he asked Cooper if he could recall that it was the gun that Truesdale had purchased for her.

"It was a small handgun, wasn't it?" Cooper answered in the affirmative.

"White shiny handle?"

"I can't remember what kind it was."

"And this was in 1987. You can't remember what kind of gun?"

"No."

Anderson got what he was after. He dressed down a witness with a bad memory. There was no reason for Caldwell to redirect. Instead, he surprised the courtroom by announcing that the Commonwealth rested its case. Upon hearing that, the judge instructed the jury to once again leave the courtroom. He then asked for any motions. Anderson was the first to speak.

"Judge, on behalf of the defendant, I would respectfully move to strike the Commonwealth's evidence in this case. I know it is a circumstantial case, but when you look at the evidence in the light most favorable to the Commonwealth, the most you have at this juncture in the proceeding is an absolute supposition of the involvement of Ms. Truesdale in this case.

"If you look at every witness that has testified, at best you have prior statements in which there are some inconsistencies in details, but there is no inconsistencies with respect to how this murder took place and how it happened."

Anderson had the judge's attention. He then began to outline his case, which was strongly built on cognition. "At best, the theory the Commonwealth has is she set out on a scheme to lead a deceitful web and that she would murder her husband on the interstate; hide the gun, the murder weapon, in her pocketbook; take the pocketbook and keep it from Jamie Martin; and they have proved that from 1967 she had a gun and in 1987 she had a gun at a service station.

"Those are the inferences that I would submit that you could draw from the evidence of the Commonwealth. You could draw the inference that the insurance was substantially more than what was stated to Officer or Special Agent Keesee. You could draw an inference that she was present at the scene.

"I guess the testimony that bothers me the most with respect is the testimony of Mr. Crouch, which was that she told him that two individuals had done this, that an individual had shot her husband and that the statement that he attributed to her, 'I didn't mean for this to happen. I didn't mean to do this.' I don't know with respect to what is meant by the substance of that statement.

"If you look at the totality of this evidence before you, I am asking you to decide that there is no reasonable evidence, and no reasonable inferences that can be drawn from the evidence that Ms. Truesdale was the murderer in this case."

Caldwell didn't get up from his chair. Instead, Betty Jo Anthony stood in front of Weckstein to advance the prosecution's case in her first action before the court. She handled herself well.

"The Commonwealth has proven through stipulation that there was a large amount of insurance from which Ms. Truesdale was the sole beneficiary. We have also shown that the time, place and means were available to her and we have indicated her conduct. She lied about the ownership of a gun. She lied about the insurance, the amount of the insurance.

"She said repeatedly that she didn't mean to do this. She changed the location of the crime from one officer to another, changed the manner in which the crime was committed. The Commonwealth's position is that time, place, means, conduct and motive. Taking all the evidence in the light most favorable to the Commonwealth with all the inferences that can be drawn, it points to the defendant's guilt enough to make this a question of fact for the jury."

Anderson was given the opportunity to further strike that the case be dismissed. He made a final plea.

"It is the prima facie evidence and what inferences they can draw, that there are no facts, either individually or cumulative, that raises more than a supposition, and that is not the standard. I respectfully ask that the case be struck."

Anderson was hoping for a favorable decision. He wouldn't have to call any witnesses. He didn't want Ms. Truesdale to appear on the witness stand. But she would have to if Weckstein refused to dismiss the case.

"The judge is not to weigh the evidence," explained Weckstein. The judge is not to decide upon the credibility of the evidence. The judge must, however, strike the evidence if it appears conclusively to him that he would be compelled to set aside a jury verdict of guilty."

"I will overrule the motion to strike. I believe that the traditional trilogy, motive, means and opportunity. The motive, time, place, means and conduct have sufficient evidence for the case to go forward."

Anderson was taken by surprise. He felt strongly about a strike. Weckstein asked if he wished to present evidence. "Yes," he answered. "But this is a bit earlier than we expected. Could I have about fifteen minutes to sort it out?"

After the recess, Anderson was ready with his first witness. He was going to start with Angela Pugh, a name not familiar to anyone in the courtroom. Except to Frances Truesdale. Angela was her daughter from her first marriage, and nobody knew or heard of her. Anderson was taking the maternal route, showing the jury that Angela maintained a relationship with her mother since she left in 1986 and moved away with her two children to King, North Carolina.

"Would you describe to the ladies and gentlemen of the jury what that relationship has been?"

"My relationship with my mother has been tight. We have enjoyed talking and going through things, and mamma helped me raise my children. I was working two jobs and going to school, and mamma kept the kids. She kept them at night for me to work. She kept them for me to go to school. Her and Pop would keep the kids."

"When you say 'Pop,' who are you referring to?"

"My stepfather, Jerry Truesdale."

"Did you enjoy a good relationship with him?"

"Pop was like a statue. Whenever my kids wanted breakfast, he would run them to the Biscuitville. When my ex-husband and I went to court, Pop and Mamma both came and they both talked me into moving because of my mental state, having gone through a divorce and all, my in-laws living next to me. I needed to get away, and they talked me into staying with them until I could get on my feet. We always had family together, and on Sundays we were all at the house."

Anderson remained on the family theme. He asked Angela to describe the relationship that existed between Jerry and Frances. Angela was only too willing to do so.

"Mamma and Pop were tight. They knew everything each one of them did. They did everything together. When we had Christmas, they bought all the Christmas presents together. We were laughing about Bill's bicycle. He wanted a ten speed, and Pop said, 'Of course, me and your mamma had to buy a twelve speed because we wanted the best for him.' They always did things together.

"I know when Pop first talked about going back into trucking, Mamma said, 'I'm not going up there every weekend.' She said she had work to do; she had to help Russell and Jody with the station, but she was up there every weekend. I don't remember a one she wasn't."

"How would you describe their affection towards each other?"

"They would cuddle every now and then, but Mom and Pop were really quite personal with their feelings. They never fussed in front of none of us. They weren't the type of people who would kiss in public because Pop just didn't believe in stuff like that."

"Was your mother a flamboyant or exuberant spender of money?"

"My mother sacrificed for the filling station and she sacrificed if little Jerry needed a car part, and she sacrificed if Pop needed something. She wore the same pair of blue jeans every other day. She never bought any clothes. She sacrificed."

Anderson was painting a loving family scene all right.

Betty Jo Anthony handled the cross-examination, her very first time before the jury. She was brief. She realized she couldn't get a daughter to say anything damaging about a mother and she didn't even try. Instead, she made two points.

"Ms. Pugh, you said that they were together in most things. Did they do their financial planning together?"

"That is something most of the time was done in private. I couldn't tell you that. I heard them talking about, 'Well, we are going to buy this,' or 'We are going to do that.' That was something that I just wasn't around that much."

"You said that they frowned on displays of emotion and that they were a very together couple. Would it surprise you to know that they were cursing at each other going down the road on April 21, 1988?"

"No, it doesn't surprise me because lots of time people curse at each other going down the road. I mean normal people do."

Anderson turned to Gene Deal next. He had been the Truesdale's neighbor for fourteen years. But he was more than that. Anderson felt his rank as a major, active in the North Carolina National Guard, would impress the jury, especially in his praise of the Truesdales. Deal had met them through their son Randy when he moved to Winston-Salem in September 1974 and over the years developed a long-lasting friendship.

"I would consider Jerry one of my best friends," Deal told the jury.

Anderson then directed Deal to the morning of April 21, 1988, when he arrived at Roanoke Memorial Hospital. He got there early, around eight o'clock, with Frances's youngest son, Jerry, and he was later introduced to Barry Keesee. Anderson asked him to describe to the jury his observations of Frances when he got there.

"It was a very pitiful scene. It was something like I have never experienced before in my life. She was visibly upset. She just did not really know how to handle the situation. It was obvious she had been crying."

Deal then described how Keesee, later in the morning, asked Frances to go back with him to the crime scene. He also asked Deal and one of the sons to accompany her. Deal felt that Frances explained to Keesee what actually happened in rather good detail, and he remembered that the officer took a tremendous amount of photographs.

They had been gone over an hour when Frances asked Keesee if she could go back to the hospital and see her husband. But he said that they had one more place to go, and Keesee took them to a Ford dealership to look at a Ford Granada. He wanted to make certain that Frances could identify the car because she had distinctly remembered seeing the word *Granada* on the back of the car. Keesee went in and came back out, declaring that the word *Granada* was not written on the back of any of the Fords.

"During this time, Frances had asked several times to go back to the hospital and asked if he could do this another time," said Deal. "I thought it was rather cruel. Later, Keesee indicated to me in a telephone conversation that he had seen one Ford with the word Granada on it."

In another phone call, Keesee called Deal in May and said that he would like to see the van again. Anderson asked Deal to explain fully what happened next.

"He asked me to bring the van and he asked me to bring a .25-caliber pistol they had looked at the first day. He indicated to me that they had not fired the weapon and that he needed the weapon back for a test. I retrieved the weapon from Frances, along with the van from the second-oldest son, Randy, and proceeded to the Virginia–North Carolina line and met Mr. Keesee there.

"He looked at the van thoroughly. He looked at the weapon, gave me a receipt for it, took a lot of pictures of the van, took pictures of me and we departed after about forty-five minutes.

"He made me feel extremely uncomfortable and I have kept this from the family until today. He had me sit in the driver's seat. He asked me to look in the direction of where the passenger would be sitting. He told me he was trying to approximate the angle the weapon was fired.

"He also took his finger and pointed it at the back of my neck, right where the bullet was supposed to have gone in and [I] felt extremely uncomfortable with this. I just felt that was something they should have done earlier."

Anderson liked what Deal was telling the jury. He was nearing the end of his questioning. He got Deal to relate how upset Frances was at the hospital and how distasteful it was for Keesee to conduct an experiment with him involved. Finally, Anderson wanted Deal to talk openly about Frances and Jerry's relationship, and he complied in glowing terms. And like a military man, he was well versed.

"I am trying to think of the right wording. Ideal is not the proper word. Maybe extremely compatible, a family that has four adopted sons and one natural son by the two parents, and had I not known this, I would never had known it.

"They did things together as a family who were extremely happy, where the husband worked and took care of his family the way he was supposed to do."

Anderson couldn't have scripted it better. Deal made a convincing witness, more so than Frances's daughter, Angela. He was pleased and convinced that Deal made an impression on the jury. It was left to Betty Jo Anthony for the cross-examination, and her challenge wouldn't be easy. As an army man, Deal was loyal, just as two buddies would be in a foxhole.

Anthony opened with Frances Truesdale's weekly travel to Pennsylvania to be with her husband. She wanted to know how long that had been going on at the time of his death. The major spoke firmly, just like any army officer would.

"Quite frequently. I mean this has been almost four years, ma'am, and I tried to put it together in my memory how long he'd been working in Pennsylvania before his death, and I could not determine that. I know she went up frequently. I cannot give you an exact number of times. I just don't know."

The prosecutor then showed her acumen in getting Deal to admit that Keesee carried out his investigation professionally with a long-worded question. She framed the question so that Deal would answer affirmatively. Still, he did so somewhat unassured.

"On the day you left the hospital to go with Agent Keesee and the defendant and her son out to try to reconstruct what she claimed happened, after you visited the rest station and the side of the road, would it be fair to say that Ms. Truesdale was saying what all happened and Agent Keesee was trying to re-create that as best he could?"

"I would say, yes."

It was getting late in the afternoon, and there wasn't much time for another witness, especially Frances Truesdale. Anderson was saving her for tomorrow, and there wouldn't be an empty seat in Judge Weckstein' s courtroom.

16

A SEED OF HATE

There was no morning session as dawn broke on the third and possibly the final day of Frances Truesdale's murder case. Judge Weckstein scheduled the proceedings for the afternoon, which enabled him to attend the funeral of a colleague's mother. The extra time allowed Anderson to shape his defense around Frances's character, and he would do it through family members. There wasn't an empty seat in the room as an appreciative Weckstein offered his sentiments for the delay.

"I appreciate you accommodating me to enable me to attend my colleague's mother's funeral this morning, and I appreciate the consideration on the part of Ms. Truesdale and the lawyers."

Next, Weckstein looked at the jurors.

"I should ask you, now that we have been this long in recess, there have been newspaper stories, and I suspect there have been radio and television stories, have any of you read, seen or heard anything in the public media about this case?"

The jury answered negatively.

Anderson's first witness made his way to the stand. He was James Ivey, Frances's brother-in-law, married to her sister, Jenny. Ivey had an outstanding résumé. He had been a police officer in Virginia and North Carolina before spending six years in the army as a criminal investigator. Since 1987, he had been a senior special agent with the Office of the Inspector General in Washington. He and Keesee had a lot in common.

Ivey received a phone call on April 21, 1988, from Frances's second-oldest son, Randall, informing him that his father had been involved in an accident and was seriously injured. Ivey suspected that it was a traffic accident since Randall didn't go into any details. It wasn't until later that night when Randall called a second time that he learned that Jerry had been shot. Two days later, Ivey and his wife drove to Winston-Salem to attend Jerry Truesdale's funeral.

"How did you find your sister-in-law at the time?" asked Anderson.

"I found her very distraught, very upset, not her normal self," responded Ivey.

It didn't take Ivey long to establish a rapport with Keesee, especially after disclosing to him his background. During their phone conversation from the hospital, Keesee sought Ivey's help. He asked him to talk to his sister-in-law to discover if any more details could be learned that would help in the investigation. Ivey was more than willing to help but only since he was asked. He made it a point to tell Keesee that he didn't want to interfere with his work.

After speaking with Frances, Ivey made another call to Keesee. "Look, my sister-in-law is very adamant about what information she has given you, the partial license plate, the fact that she feels very confident it was a New York plate, the description of the car and the description of the individuals," said Ivey.

"What observations, if any, did you make of Frances during the week after the funeral?" Anderson wanted to know.

"My sister-in-law was not herself. She is a very strong type individual. I know her to be a mother who raised five young boys with a husband who was on the road quite a bit as a truck driver, and she did a hell of a job. Anybody who can do that has to be a strong person.

"This was not the person I knew. I was her escort at the funeral service. This woman, my sister-in-law, was very much broken up, shaking, crying, extremely distraught and upset. I rode with her in the limousine to the burial site, same thing. We sat there and as my brother-in-law, Jerry, was being laid to rest, she went totally to pieces. It took me about five minutes to get her to get out of the chair. This woman was not the woman that I had known in previous times."

For the second straight day, Betty Jo Anthony handled the cross-examination. She reaffirmed Keesee's credentials as a professional investigator who did his job.

"In dealing with Agent Keesee, did he speak with you in a professional manner and cooperate in the things that you suggested?" inquired Anthony.

"Yes, very much so, ma'am," Ivey quickly answered.

Anderson wasn't quite ready for Frances yet, but he was choreographing the moment. It was time for the children to paint Frances as a loving, caring mother and wife. One by one they followed each other on the witness stand as if on cue, amplifying for the jury her benignity. Anderson introduced William, the oldest son, first, and he was followed in succession by Jody, Randy and Wendell.

In glowing terms, they vocalized what a thoughtful mother she had been and what a devoted wife she was until Jerry's death, how she left every weekend to drive to Pennsylvania to be with him. Frances and Jerry were inseparable in their eyes. William described how his mother "went to pieces" when he first saw her at the hospital the night of the shooting. "I never seen her like that before," he remarked. However, when William said his mother never left the hospital to accompany Keesee later that morning, Anderson took him in another direction.

"How was your mother when you went back to Winston-Salem from the hospital?"

"She was a basket case. She stayed in her room, or she would sit in the living room and she never said much. She asked to go to the cemetery every day, but she wouldn't go alone. I took her a couple of times, and I just couldn't do it anymore. It was too much emotionally."

It was Randy who made an admission that Anderson wasn't expecting when asked about the relationship of his mother and father.

"They were lovers to the point where it would make me sick," he exclaimed. "I would tell them to get a room sometimes, and it was just all the time."

Randy's disclosure was a complete contradiction to what Angela Pugh had said the day before. She had described how personal Jerry and Frances were in their feeling of emotion. In Angela's own words, "They weren't the type of people who would kiss in public. Their private feelings were private feelings. Pop just didn't believe in stuff like that. He didn't believe in showing your feelings in public."

Apparently, Frances and Jerry were more libidinous than they had been portrayed. Anthony took advantage of that in cross-examining Randy.

"You said that they had a relationship that they might need to have a room, that would include being physically close to each other?"

"Well, you get out in public and they would be kissing each other and stuff. I guess it would embarrass me and I would make comments to them."

It didn't get by the prosecution that Anderson got each of the four boys to speak unkindly about the Truesdale family. Each of them felt uncomfortable being around them when they visited one another, which wasn't often. William even said that they really never much cared for his mother. He added that Pop would be angry driving home because of the way that they treated Mamma or the boys.

Randy also expressed his feelings about the Truesdales. He said they all felt like outsiders when they went to see them. He mentioned that very seldom any of them would come to North Carolina to visit. And he added that his dad didn't have much to do with them because of that.

Anderson was giving the jury something to think about. He was planting a seed of hate in their minds. The Truesdale family in Winnsboro didn't like Frances, showed her no love, no affection, not even to her children. Jerry's murder would be a perfect time to get back at her. Anderson masterfully played the hate card.

There weren't any more children left for Anderson to call upon to convey the maternal and wifely attributes of Frances Truesdale. It was time for her to appear before the court in her own self-defense and be heard in the arena in which she was presented.

But Weckstein suggested a timely recess. The court would have to wait fifteen minutes for Frances Truesdale' s appearance, which they anticipated would be dramatic.

17

FRANCES TESTIFIES

Judge Clifford Weckstein was fully prepared for the compelling testimony Frances Truesdale was expected to deliver when her defense attorney Tony Anderson called her to the witness stand in the afternoon of the third day of the gripping trial. In an unprecedented, if not rare procedure, he switched courtrooms, opting for a larger one at the far end of the courthouse. A swelling crowd, that included a plethora of media, had gathered for Frances's testimony, and Weckstein, observing the situation, ultimately decided for the change during the recess.

When court was reconvened, Weckstein explained why the unfamiliar new courtroom was a necessity. And he did so with flair in a colorful oratory. But before the jury was seated, he elucidated his action courteously and directly to Anderson.

"Does it throw you off stride to do that just at the time Ms. Truesdale is taking the stand?" he asked Anderson. The defense attorney smiled and responded with a quip that drew some laughter from the spectators.

"Judge, it doesn't throw me off stride. I have been accused many times of not knowing my right from my left, and this won't be any exception."

Even Weckstein cracked a smile at Anderson's humor. He then ordered the bailiff to bring in the jury and explained to them why they were sitting in a new courtroom.

The entire courtroom watched the defendant, Frances Ann Scott Truesdale, neatly attired in peach-colored suit, walk to the witness stand. The trial had reached its zenith with her appearance. She always enjoyed being the center of attention, only this time the leading lady of the drama was accused of a nefarious murder, a role she never expected to play. This was her libretto, and she was conditioned to spend as much time telling her story in establishing her person as a devoted wife and a loving mother.

And Anderson provided the background. He had Frances recite the date of her marriage to Jerry Truesdale, the excessive number of moves from South Carolina to North Carolina, living in cities such as Greenville, Greensboro and Kennersville, Pennsylvania, all within a year and a half in 1973. He got Frances to reveal that all during that time she was going through a rugged adjustment.

She supported her husband's decision to drive a truck, which took him away from home. Her testimony played out this way: how busy she was, almost to the point of being overwhelmed, in raising five boys; school preparedness; Little League participation; and all the other responsibilities required of a mother of five while her husband was gone anywhere from eighteen to forty-eight hours, even as long as six days, before he earned three or four days off. After Anderson finished with the mother-wife melodrama, he wanted the jury to know of her husband's injury and asked Frances to portray it.

"He hit his head in the top of a Pilot truck February 5, 1982, and was out of work for two weeks. They tried to convince him it was muscle spasms. He went to chiropractors, but things got worse. He was having headaches and was thinking the worst.

"He thought he had a brain tumor and he arranged to see a neurosurgeon. He lost control of a lot of stability. His right side became unstable. He would stagger. The last week in September 1983, they put him in a hospital and operated."

Frances was giving a dramatic account of Jerry's condition. Anderson wanted more to arouse sympathy from the jury members, and he led Frances into going further.

"In 1983, did he attain a disability rating from Pilot and not drive a truck for a period of time?" he asked.

Having locked the jury on a picture of a disabled husband, Anderson pushed further. He wanted Frances to tell how her husband had to undergo a rehabilitation period in an effort to complete his recovery.

"He had conferences, they did tests and they arranged for him to go to different pain clinics in an effort to lower his medication through bio-feedback. They were telling him that if he would take the things, he had an interest in other than trucks, he could make a living. A service station was suggested, and we looked at several that were available. Jerry worked in one for a period of thirty days and after that we were the proud owners of a new service station, in March or April of 1986."

Anderson wanted to make a point in the purchase. "How much did you and Jerry pay for the business?"

"Twenty thousand dollars, cash!"

The service station purchase wasn't the answer for Jerry's rehabilitation. Frances said that this new direction didn't fulfill him. He wasn't happy in not being behind the wheel of a truck. Finally, one day, he told Frances that he decided on going back to work for Pilot.

With Jerry back on the road, doing what he liked best, Frances disclosed the agreement she made with him. She would help run the service station with her two sons and she would spend weekends with him. She made it a point to emphasize to the jury that she didn't miss a single weekend in being with her husband.

"We were very happy even with having a little efficiency apartment. No kids, nobody around. We would just get in the van or the Corvette and go anywhere, New York, Ohio. I had never seen the Canadian border until then."

Anderson was not ready for the vital portion of Frances's testimony. He wanted her to tell, in her own words, exactly what she experienced that fateful night of April 21, 1988. And he didn't want her to hurry but relate every detail no matter how small or insignificant. Clutching a tissue, Frances began her oration, one that would last for two and a half hours.

"On Wednesday evening, we had slept all day. About eight o'clock, we had decided that we were going to go home together. He had two weeks' vacation that was to start on Sunday, but he could take the rest of the week off. We stopped by the terminal to pick up his paycheck. He called the service station and told Little Jerry, 'Your mamma and I are coming in.' We then went to Shoney's, ate and headed south on 81 out of Pennsylvania.

"When we approached a rest area, Jerry said he had to go to the bathroom. We went into the restroom together. He went into the men's on the right and me the ladies on the left. Jerry always told me to peek out the door before exiting to make sure he was there waiting. I pulled the door open and spotted his shirt, proceeded on out and we started down the sidewalk.

"There were two young men coming out of the restroom. I thought or assumed that he knew them, only because of the fact that they were smiling, and it was almost like they had just spoke or something. I asked, 'who are they,' and he said, 'Goddam dead beats.' He didn't explain but he looked mad and I didn't persist any further.

"We continued towards our parked vehicle. Those young men caught up with us as we got to the front of the van. One of them touched his right elbow and said, 'Lay it on me, man. Just hold my watch. Lay it on me.' Almost without a jerk, Jerry's arm came up and struck the young man in the mouth.

"I just froze, panic stricken. I expected them to lunge on him, but the boy didn't move. He just looked at him. I then jumped into the driver's seat of the van. I assumed that since I drove in, I would drive out.

"He said, 'Get the hell over. Get out of the way.' It was the sound of voice that you knew to move instantly, and I got into the captain's chair by sliding into it. He backed out of the parking space and started out of the rest area.

"I was crying, and he was cussing. He said things like, 'Goddamn dead beats and Yankees. They're getting in that New York Ford.' I glanced over and the boys were walking towards a black car, and I said, RUD.

"We proceeded on our way around Roanoke. We referred to it as the beltway, 81 and 581. We came through some construction and after we got out of the construction there wasn't any more streetlights. That same car swung in front of us into the lane we were in. Jerry had to brake, and I started screaming at him to keep going because it was the same black car. He swung into the left lane and accelerated. They swung right in behind us and they were so close that their lights were inside the van.

"Within a few seconds he slammed on the brakes and said, 'I've had enough of this shit. This is stopping.' He had his arm on the door. The door opened. His body went that away. He was stepping out and I had ahold of his right arm and my knees in his seat screaming. I could just visualize one of them hitting him."

Frances began to sob. She took a deep breath and continued. "A hand with a gun in it came inside with us. I could see a flash. I could hear it. I could smell it. It was all very fast, and Jerry's head went forward, and that boy just stood there. Jerry's neck was bleeding, and I had a pillow and pushed it into it. I put my foot on the accelerator and I was heading into the median and couldn't turn the steering wheel because he was on it. I went into the grass again.

"I stopped my foot on the brake and I pulled him in one motion, in a panic, down and out of the way. All I could think of was going home and I started thinking hospital and I knew there wasn't one that away. I started looking for somewhere I could make a U-turn.

"I got back into the lighted area and I knew there were hospitals on both sides of me. I didn't know where to get off because there wasn't any hospital signs. By then I was talking to myself, mamma you can do it. He always told me I could do it. Everything I went to do, he would say, 'Mamma you can do it. Be calm, mamma, you can do it.'

"I started hollering on the CB. 'I need to get to the hospital. My husband has been shot in the neck.' Somebody answered, 'Where are you?' I told him I didn't know. I remembered something about Hershberger Road, and he told me to get off there.

"I stopped and a man pulled up and I got out of the van. At first, I thought he was a policeman because he had some kind of uniform on. My legs wouldn't hold me up, and he held me up. I started telling him RUD, R-U-D, help me remember RUD.

"There were more policemen than I have ever thought of in my life and an ambulance. There were police officers everywhere and they were talking to me and they cut Jerry's shirt off. They put him in the ambulance, and they hooked me in the front seat, and we went to the hospital and Jerry didn't go home with us."

Frances wiped tears from her eyes. It was a traumatic ordeal, almost surreal, in relating publicly for the first time in front of a full courtroom the shooting of her husband. Judging by the look of the jury, she had done well. Anderson couldn't have asked for more from her.

Instead, it was time for him to posture Keesee as an antagonist, an investigator who was cold and relentless to the point of not being compassionate to a traumatized wife who was sitting in a small room in the intensive care unit of a hospital where he found her, pale and trembling, waiting to see if her husband would live or die. Frances became irked at the mention of Keesee's name when she started talking about the very first time she met him in the hospital.

"Right off the bat he told me that he was with the Virginia State Police and that he had just left the van and said, 'I took care of your baby.' I asked him what baby, and he said, 'Your dog.' He didn't like my reaction. I told him I didn't like the dog but my husband loved that dog to death.

"He kept telling me, 'Lady, you have to calm down. You have got to tell me things so that I will know what to do.' A nurse then asked me if I wanted any kind of medication? But Agent Keesee told me if I could just hold on and give him some information that it would be better. And I did.

"A lot of things he said to me was reassuring, like, 'Now you and I are going to solve this problem and the doctors are going to take care of Jerry. They are the best and they are working on him now.' I asked him if I could see Jerry and he said not right now that he had to talk to me while things were fresh in my mind.

"He started backtracking, and we went over details over and over for hours. When Randy came through the door, I was never so glad to see my kids in my life. I again asked Keesee if I could see Jerry, and he said there were a lot of things that we had to go over.

"A doctor came into the room to inform me that the bullet was not in Jerry's neck, but it was in his head and there was a blood clot. He needed permission to operate. A Black minister sat down beside me and patted me and said, 'Don't decide yourself. Let God decide.'

"I kept saying that I wanted to see Jerry, but he said, 'When we finish up.' Then a man came in, and he wanted me to start piecing these boys' pictures together, their faces. Agent Keesee said, 'When we get through with this, I will let you go see Jerry and get some rest.' I got to see Jerry, but they told me I couldn't stay long. I just laid my head on the pillow and just snuggled up to him."

Frances broke down again. She covered her eyes and began sobbing. There were a few others in the crowded courtroom who also wiped their eyes. Frances's tears got to them.

Anderson could only hope that she got to the jury, too. With a teary Frances to help him, Anderson continued his purge of Keesee, beginning at the rest area the morning she went there with him, Gene Deal and her son Russell.

"Agent Keesee asked me, 'Where did you park?' and I pointed, and he parked there. He got out, walked around and made comments like, 'Yeah, there are the trash cans where you said they were.' As we were pulling out, he said, 'Now, when you got along right here, they were where?' And I pointed.

"All that day he kept telling me I didn't see the word Granada on the tail end of that car. He went into one of the places that we went to and he said that the Ford people there said the word Granada wasn't on the tail end. He started chit-chatting with all of us and as we were going along, he would point out where different things were. I doubt if I remembered two minutes after what he said. Then he started telling me about three bodies that were found, and somebody's body had been found in a rock quarry and he was working on those cases." Anderson used that opportunity of what Frances just described to show no remorse on Keesee's part.

Then Anderson explored the life insurance angle. The $285,000 windfall was prominent in the minds of the jury. It certainly represented a viable motive for murder. Anderson had to address it, and he did so directly. He wanted to show the jury that he didn't intend to ignore it or treat it lightly.

"Did Agent Keesee make any inquiries of you at the hospital as to the amount of life insurance your husband had?"

"When Agent Keesee had me in that little room, he asked me if anyone had taken out any large life insurance policies on my husband recently? I told him no, and he said, 'Of course, you haven't,' and I said no. Then he asked, 'Do you know how much life insurance your husband had?' I said, Jerry always said he had $35,000 worth of life insurance."

"Did Agent Keesee call you by phone and ask you a question about your husband's life insurance proceeds?"

"Approximately the last week of May or the first week of June. I had company and I asked him if he could call me back later or if I could call him. He said, 'It is just one question. I just want to know, did you tell me in the emergency room that Jerry had $35,000 worth of life insurance,' and I said, yes, sir, I did say that. Can I call you back later, or can you call me, and he said, 'No, that is all I wanted to know.'

"That bothered me, and I went to Janet Pauca's office the next morning because he wouldn't let me answer his question later. Janet is my friend, too, and I told her I needed a list of the insurance. She ran a copy off. I had an envelope that I had just gotten a note from Keesee, and she copied the address and sent this information to Agent Keesee. He never, ever got back to me about it.

Having established his client's knowledge of the insurance, it was time for Anderson to illustrate how munificent Frances was with the proceeds, that she didn't keep the money for herself. She was portrayed as a caring mother who loved her children.

"Please relate to the jury what, if anything, you did with these proceeds."

"The kids got some of it. I paid my house payment. I paid my homeowner' s insurance and taxes. I paid my car payment. I paid my car insurance. I gave William money for a Corvette that his dad had promised to help him get. I paid off Russell's bills and his vehicles so he could qualify for his home loan.

"I paid some bills for Jody. I gave Jerry the money for the 1969 Corvette that him and his daddy were looking for. I paid off the truck that little Jerry bought impulsively without realizing they were charging him 16 percent interest because of his age."

Frances was on a spree and she kept rattling off the bill payments, one right after the other. It was just what Anderson hoped she would do, in rapid fashion to dramatize how fast the money Frances received was being spent on her children. Anderson knew what the answer to the next question was, but he wanted the jury to hear it. Once again, he was making Keesee the fall guy.

"Is that restaurant still in business?"

"No, sir. When Agent Keesee came around asking questions about me in September, word spread like wildfire that I was being investigated for the murder of my husband. I invested money all of 1988 until December 30, when Jerry and Russell wanted out of the service station. They couldn't stand it anymore, and I couldn't either. It was costing me two or three thousand dollars a month to keep the doors open. I closed the doors on December 30 and paid off all the debts."

"Do you have any of the proceeds from the insurance policy left at this time?"

"About $4,000."

Anderson convincingly presented what he set out to do. He verified that Frances didn't spend the money only on herself but instead gave so much of it to her children that she barely had anything left for herself. All that was left for him to do now was to remove any doubts about a gun that had always been associated with his client.

"Did there come a time in 1987 when Jerry Truesdale purchased a handgun for you?"

"One of the subcontractors came into the service station, one that I called carpetbagger, because every time he came to work, he was selling something. I don't know who brought up the conversation, he or Jerry, but Jerry purchased a small, shiny gun with a pearl handle that was so big.

"Jerry walked up to me and said, 'Mamma, do you think you can learn how to handle this'? I said sure, and he bought it. He put it in a little brown zipper thing and put it in the van. He told me to make sure I had it in the motel room if I was by myself and to keep it laying on the front seat in that case."

"Is that the gun that was in your possession that you advised Officer Keesee about on April 21, 1988?"

Anderson then got Frances to say that the very same gun was in her possession that she advised Officer Keesee about on the night of the killing. Then he was ready for his one final question, one that could very well determine the verdict of the jury. He was deliberate and enunciated clearly the question he finally waited to ask.

"Ms. Truesdale, I want you to look at the ladies and the gentlemen of this jury and I want you to answer this question for me. Did you on April 21, 1988, intentionally, willfully and deliberately with premeditation shoot and kill your husband?"

Frances didn't waver. She answered firmly through her tears.

"No, I did not. I did not kill my husband."

At exactly ten minutes before the hour of five, the curtain came down on Frances's performance. Anderson had no more questions. The prosecution would have to wait until tomorrow.

18

TROUBLE REMEMBERING

Surprisingly, the Commonwealth's lead attorney, Donald Caldwell, did not step forward on the fourth day of the trial to cross-examine Frances Truesdale. Instead, he trusted his assistant, Betty Jo Anthony, to handle the vital procedure, which filled the Roanoke County Courthouse's biggest courtroom. It was a strategic maneuver. The female members of the jury would be more amenable to having a woman prosecutor challenge a female defendant. And Betty Jo was worthy of the task.

She didn't hesitate in opening with the gun issue. However, she couldn't get Frances to admit possessing the .25 caliber in her purse. Frances denied repeatedly the claims of Barbara Martin, Betty Ruth McGinnis and William Cooper that they saw her with such a gun. She also answered no, when asked if she recalled the day in 1967 when she, Betty Ruth and another woman named Cookie confronted Ben Branham in an adulterous affair in his own house with a gun in her hand. Even though she never acknowledged what others had testified, Frances was suspect by her denials, and Anthony's questions were effective.

Frances also testified that she didn't remember telling Agent Keesee the night her husband was killed that she didn't own a gun, was afraid of them and didn't know how to use them. When Anthony pressed further, Frances admitted telling Keesee that the pistol was in the van.

"I don't understand what you are trying to get me to say," claimed Frances, shaking her head.

"I'm not trying to get you to say anything, Ms. Truesdale," Anthony quickly answered. "These are not trick questions. I just want the jury to understand what the truth is. My question was if you told Agent Keesee that you didn't know anything about guns, you didn't have a gun and you were afraid of guns; he said that you told him you had a .25 caliber in the van. I am asking you, did you make that statement to him?"

"I don't remember making the statement."

Anthony was determined to validate gun possession. She confronted the defendant with the fact that she obtained not one, but two, permits to carry pistols.

"If you didn't have a second gun, why would you need a second permit?"

"They explained to me that in the state of North Carolina that two were available, and they suggested taking them."

Anthony then referred to a deposition that Frances gave on January 30, 1990, in Winston-Salem in which she was asked if she could learn to use the weapon that her husband bought in 1987 in which she replied she could. Frances couldn't remember saying that.

Next, Anthony asked Frances if she could identify the gun the night of the killing when she observed it up close in the assailant's hand. Another no.

"Then how could you tell Ann Letrick in the hospital while your husband was still alive with the bullet in his head that it was a .22?"

"I could not have told her."

Meticulously, Anthony traced Frances's weekly trips to Pennsylvania to be with her husband, and Frances was all too willing to comply in showing the jury what a devoted wife she was. Frances put the number of trips at ninety-six in one year, even describing the four weekends she missed. Anthony led her effectively and then strongly made her points to the jury.

She emphasized that since Frances was in the service station business, she should have stopped at one that she had passed at least ninety-six times to get help the night her husband was shot. She also got her to admit that she missed pulling over to the Parkway Restaurant, which she was familiar with, missing five exits in the process before getting off on Hershberger Road.

"And on those ninety-six trips that you had previously made, you had seen those exits, had you not?"

"Yes."

"The hospital has big letters across the top and sits almost touching the interstate, and you didn't get off at that exit?"

"I didn't find that exit."

That, too, played well for the prosecution with the jury. How could someone who drove past the very spot almost one hundred times not recognize a hospital practically standing on the highway with the big word

Parkway Hospital easily seen by a motorist? Frances wasn't very convincing with that part of her testimony.

Anthony turned next to the statement Frances gave to Keesee on September 18, 1989, in her home. Yet Frances couldn't remember telling him that one of the assailants had on a white T-shirt, but she didn't know what the other one was wearing. In Frances's own words, "I didn't look that good and I don't know how tall or what weight." She was also not sure the pair were military personnel but looked like, as she described them, "seminary students."

Once again Frances had difficulty remembering, this time, the testimony she gave Keesee in describing the scene at the rest area. Anthony read it to her from page five of the transcript after her husband struck one of the assailants near the van.

"I figured they would lunge. That boy didn't bat an eye; he just stood there, and I said, 'let's go,' and I just automatically jumped in. Then he said, 'Goddamn it,' and I remember him cussing and shoving. I'm pulling on him and he was pushing and shoving me to get me to get in the van. Wouldn't you be scared if you just popped somebody? People are crazy."

Anthony looked up from the transcript. "Is that the way it was? Was he angry or was he frightened?"

"I don't remember this exact conversation."

Anthony went to her table and returned with a deposition that Frances had given in Winston-Salem on January 30, 1990. She turned to page eighty-five and read out loud lines five, six, seven and eight.

"Do you recall the examiner asking you the question, 'I take it by this point you had come to a stop'? Answer: 'Yes, sir.' Question: 'Right in the middle of the road?' Answer: 'Yes, sir.' Question: 'And he opened the door?' Answer: 'He was opening the door.' Do you recall saying that?"

"Not word for word," hedged Frances.

Anthony raised her voice. "But this was under oath and now you are telling the jury that you can't swear where you were stopped, but that day you swore to it."

"I don't know the exact words I used that day. I still insist my husband just stopped and we were in the inside lane."

"And that is your testimony today under oath?"

"Yes, ma'am."

Once again Frances had a memory lapse when Anthony began asking her about the insurance claims. She denied that she kept the policies in a shoebox. But when Anthony reminded her that is what she testified to the insurance company, Frances still couldn't recall saying so. She couldn't even remember calling Veterans Life on May 2, 1988, to claim the $100,000. She had a difficult time recalling filling out various insurance forms with the other companies when Anthony challenged her about misrepresenting the claims.

"When Agent Keesee asked you how much life insurance you had, in order to divert suspicion from yourself, instead of telling him the truth, you played a word game and told him that Jerry always said $35,000."

"I did not do it for that purpose. It was just habitual, saying what he said."

Anthony was miffed. "Habitually saying what he said! So, the man who is trying to find the people that you claim shot your husband asked you a question about insurance, and you didn't give it your full attention; you just said Jerry says $35,000?"

Anthony wasn't quite finished. She asked Frances to look over some insurance forms she signed. Then she posed her question. "The form that you signed and sent in, you signed that these statements were true. Is that right?"

"I don't remember that paper?"

Anthony kept her composure, but her voice reflected anger. "But you signed it. Isn't it true that you are telling this jury only partial truths?"

"No, ma'am. I am telling this jury everything that I can remember."

That was enough for Anthony.

Anderson performed his redirect quickly, playing on the sympathy of the jury panel. He asked his client to describe what happened after she returned home to Winston-Salem following the funeral. Frances replied she entered a hospital named Charter Mandella. However, it wasn't your everyday normal hospital.

"Would you tell the ladies and gentlemen of the jury what type of hospital it is?"

"It is a private psychiatric hospital."

"Could you give us the dates?"

Frances's memory didn't fail her. She may not have remembered everything the prosecution asked just minutes before, but she had no problem delivering the dates of her hospital stay.

"I know the dates were May 13 to May 23," answered Frances, almost on cue.

Anderson got Frances to relate how she needed help from Leslie Dorset, a neighbor, to conduct her affairs prior to entering the psychiatric hospital. During this period, Frances repeated that she didn't remember the phone calls or the papers she signed for the insurance claims.

Anderson then worked on the gun theory. Frances again claimed that her husband purchased a weapon for her.

"He bought a .38 revolver during the trucking strike," recalled Frances. "I don't remember the dates, but he nicknamed it Mr. Rossie. He bought it from my brother-in-law, a police officer. He also bought a small gun, I think it was a .22, years ago but I don't know what year."

When Anderson had Frances testify that she didn't have any other weapon in her possession other than the .25 automatic pistol on April 21, 1988, he touched on the insurance claims.

Frances revealed that Union Fidelity refused to make immediate payments. Instead, with the other claim checks, she invested in a $30,000 second mortgage on her sister's house on the advice of an attorney. Frances was attracted by the 10 percent interest rate.

Anderson had one more question, and he kept it until the end in his redirect of his client. It was a lengthy one, but it required only a two-word answer.

"The gun permits that you acquired in North Carolina in August of 1988 were well after any of the events that occurred that you are being accused of that resulted in this trial this week?"

"Yes, sir."

Anthony had only a couple of significant questions in her short recross-examination. She exploited the area of the gun and deliberately focused on the .22 caliber. Frances wasn't helpful.

"I don't remember the last time I saw that," she remarked. "I remember Mr. Rossie in 1982."

"But you didn't see fit to mention these in your depositions or earlier?" pressed Anthony.

"I don't recall."

Frances exhibited another convenient memory lapse.

To reinforce the family harmony approach, Anderson called Jerry Truesdale Jr. to the stand for the first time. Being the only son from the union of Frances and Jerry, he didn't want to include him with the other four boys the day they appeared on the stand. Anderson felt that saving his testimony for last would have more of an effect on the jury.

It was the same litany as earlier: Frances, the loving wife, driving to Pennsylvania on weekends, a second honeymoon euphoria, stories the jury heard before. The night that Jerry met his mother in the hospital made an impact.

"She was hysterical, and she started screaming," said Jerry. "She started crying, hysterically screaming, saying that she tried to stop them. She grabbed ahold of me and held me and just wouldn't let me go."

Then Anderson wanted the court to hear in Jerry's own words how distraught Frances was after the funeral the week he stayed with her in Winston-Salem.

"Mamma always had a saying, 'I'll eat with Daddy.' After Daddy died, she just didn't eat. Whenever anybody would ask her to eat, she would just say, 'I'm not hungry.' She just didn't know when to eat, and she lost weight. She didn't do anything. She just stayed in the house and would go to the cemetery as many times as someone would take her because she wouldn't go by herself. Everybody took her to the cemetery, and she went there a lot. She just didn't do nothing but sit home and cry."

Further explaining his mother's mental state, Jerry acknowledged that a neighbor, Leslie Dorset, took care of the bills and wrote checks for Frances to sign.

That's all Anderson wanted, too. He rested his case.

In his rebuttal, Caldwell got Keesee to repeat that Frances remarked that her husband had only $25,000 in life insurance. He was implanting the money motive of the actual $285,000 that she would collect upon his death. He also made it a point to emphasize that Keesee never received any correspondence from Frances or her attorney on a complete accounting of the amount of life insurance due her.

Ben Branham was recalled as a rebuttal witness and almost had the courtroom in laughter. First, he couldn't remember the year he got married to Betty Ruth McGinnis and presented a time span from 1964 through 1967. He finally agreed on 1965 because he owned a 1965 Pontiac, which left several members of the audience shaking their heads.

Branham couldn't even remember the exact year he was having sex with another woman when his wife, Sandra Beasley and another woman burst into the house and caught him in bed. He confessed that his sexual encounter occurred between 1965 and 1968. However, he did remember Sandra pointing a gun at him that appeared to be a .22 caliber.

The last witness summoned by Caldwell was Julia Sowder, who was Jerry Truesdale's sister, a legal secretary in Milledgeville, Georgia. She told the court that she answered to the name of Judy to remove any confusion. Caldwell didn't waste any time in getting Judy to relate the conversation she had with Frances the first night in the hospital.

"I was under the impression that Jerry was shot at a truck stop," began Judy. "When I found out she was with Jerry, I said, 'Why are you alive? Criminals don't leave witnesses when they shoot somebody and kill them.'

"She told me that Barry Keesee had checked her already. That he had interrogated her. He had asked her questions like the date of her birth, how old she was, stupid questions like that. She also said that he checked her hands for powder burns."

"Was the issue of life insurance ever brought up?"

"Yes. She asked Diane, a friend of hers, should she tell me what a financial mess Jerry was leaving her in. He only left her $25,000 in life insurance."

Anderson attempted to portray Judy as a spiteful woman who hated Frances but didn't succeed.

"You do not like Frances Truesdale, do you?"

"She made my brother happy to start with, and that is all I could ask for. I did not have to live with her."

"My question is: You did not like Frances Truesdale, did you?"

"I can't say that I liked her nor disliked her."

Judge Weckstein gave the jury a long lunch break—until two o'clock. He wanted them to be fresh for the closing statements of both attorneys. Once again, Anderson asked for a motion to strike after the jury left, and once again Weckstein ruled against it.

The burden fell on Anderson's shoulders. It was up to him to impress the jury for a non-guilty verdict in his final oratory. And he was good at that.

19

A VERDICT

Betty Jo Anthony was the first to address the jury in final summations of the four-day trial. She would be followed by Anderson, who displayed his adroitness as a speaker, and finally Caldwell in rebuttal.

Anthony carefully elucidated to the attentive jury the characteristics of circumstantial and direct evidence, almost making it appear as if they were one and the same. When she returned to her seat, she was acknowledged with a nod from Caldwell signifying she had delivered creditably. Weckstein, giving the jury members time to absorb the Commonwealth's conclusion, ordered a ten-minute recess before hearing Anderson's remarks, which were expected to be lengthy.

Throughout the trial, Anderson handled himself with éclat. At moments, he showed skillful benignity and at times impugned several witnesses to benefit his client. He was even genteel in his mannerisms and suave in his dress, sporting a different suit each day. But now he would need all his acumen as an orator to influence the jury on a favorable decision.

He began by depicting a night of horror and hysteria, the draining emotions of a woman alone in a hospital crying over the serious condition of her husband of twenty years and living a nightmare the last four years. Having done that, he categorically outlined his defense, prefacing it by stating that on that traumatic night there was no evidence, none whatsoever, of a .22-caliber gun.

"Are we going back to 1967, to 1971, to 1975? Can we hold as accountable our own actions from that period of time? Can we say, can you collectively will your verdict as a group of one that remotely considered Ms. Truesdale had the means to intentionally and willfully and deliberately murder her husband?

"She misstated the insurance amount to Barry Keesee because Jerry said, 'Don't let people know your business. Tell them it is $35,000.' If she was doing that to avoid detection or avoid herself being detected as a murderess, why is she around? Why didn't she take that $250,000 that the Commonwealth would have you believe in and take off? This case has been pending almost four years.

"Did you see any evidence that Frances and Jerry Truesdale had a relationship with either themselves or their family in which she could survive in the world without her husband? The evidence is just the opposite of that. The evidence is that she was a wreck.

"The Commonwealth will submit to you that because she has made some inconsistent statements, because she misstated the amount of insurance on several occasions, that she is a liar; and, therefore, if she is a liar, she is a murderer.

"They don't have any evidence as to what happened on April 21. You are not tried and convicted on innuendoes, on speculation, ongoing outside of the evidence and hunting up ideas. I submit to you Frances Truesdale did not murder her husband. She looked each one of you in the eye and told you she did not murder her husband."

Anderson quickly returned to his table with a confident look and caught Frances Truesdale's eye, signifying he had done his part in trying to persuade the jury. She didn't say anything. Anderson sat in his chair, waiting for the Commonwealth's lead attorney to speak.

Caldwell explained to the jury the purpose of the rebuttal portion of the closing argument. The burden of proving the case is on the Commonwealth, he told them. And he didn't hesitate in reminding them about the inconsistencies in Frances Truesdale's testimony. He pointed to her insurance questionnaire from Union Fidelity in which she described the assailants yet couldn't give a description of them in court.

"In evaluating her credibility, you will find that it means absolutely nothing to her to sit on this stand, look you in the eye and say, 'I didn't do it.' She can do that quite easily. She has done that very easily on a number of occasions as you know.

"Here was a man who was supposedly in the driver's seat while his wife was in the seat next to him, leaning over him, through him, around him, somewhere, holding a pillow over his neck, driving and then starting to talk on the CB. Somehow, she managed to do all of these things, and yet there is no blood in the van anywhere other than the pallet area in the back of the van. That defies logic; that defies reasonable explanation.

"This woman controlled time and place. The only way we have any idea where this occurred is what she tells us. She was there; she was present. She was the only other person with Jerry Truesdale, unless you would believe that story about two, unknown assailants. Her means are proven by the fact that she had a long history of involvements with guns."

There was nothing more to be said. It had been a long day. It was 5:10 p.m. when Judge Weckstein gave his instructions to the jurors. As usual, he was clear and precise in his presentation. He offered them two choices. They could remain behind closed doors, eat dinner and then vote or wait until the next day to render their verdict. The jurors elected to remain. After they left to deliberate, Weckstein addressed the court and was stern in his remarks.

Those who waited, mostly family members and friends, heard the verdict at 9:30 p.m. Frances Truesdale sat quietly, clasping her hands. She looked straight at the jury foreman as he spoke. When he uttered the word *guilty*, she slumped in her chair in disbelief. She was stunned, her head bowed, sentenced to twenty years on a charge of second-degree murder. The nightmare she had been living the past four years turned into a death knell.

20

JUDY TRUESDALE

In a confidential letter to Fairfield County solicitor John Justice dated April 1, 1992, I.C. Handy of the Virginia State Police related that Frances Scott Truesdale, a.k.a. Sandra Beasley, was convicted for the murder of her husband, Jerry Truesdale in 1988 on February 27, 1992. During Special Agent Barry Keesee's investigation, the letter continued, he discovered that Truesdale probably killed her third husband, Ronald Beasley, on July 6, 1967, in Fairfield County, South Carolina. Along with his letter, Handy enclosed several investigative documents felt would be helpful in any investigation that might occur.

It wasn't until seven months later that an investigation finally began. On November 10, Betty Ruth McGinnis, who had worked for the Beasleys in 1967, was contacted by local Fairfield County law officials. She described Sandra as a sharp-minded, conniving woman who was masterful at manipulating others and getting what she wanted. At the time she worked for the Beasleys, she was separated from her husband, Ben Branham Jr., and living in a trailer with her friend Cookie Hennessee.

"When my cousin, Jerry Truesdale, came home from service, he came by to see me," continued Betty Ruth. "Sandra had eyes for him and immediately started to pursue a relationship with him. They would kiss each other in front of me without shame, and she often sat on his lap while Ron was in the bedroom. She was determined to have Jerry.

"Ron was helpless and had the mentality of a child, and there was no way he could have committed suicide, first by cutting his wrists and then with a shotgun. A child doesn't even know what suicide means. On the day that he supposedly shot himself, Sandra acted very strange, and it was obvious to me that she wanted me out of the house. She insisted that I take one of the boys and go to the store even though I had other things to do around the house."

Nothing more was done until Herman Young officially took office as Fairfield County sheriff in January. He had assumed his elective office earlier, in September, at the insistence of the governor, when Bubba Montgomery was removed as sheriff. Fulfilling a vow he had made at the time of Beasley's death, Young quietly and effectively continued the investigation. It took twenty-six years for the opportunity to arrive, and Young seized the moment he had waited for all those years. It took him only two months to collect enough evidence from witnesses to petition for an indictment of Sandra Beasley for the murder of her husband, Ronald Beasley.

On May 11, 1993, Young dispatched Robert Byrd of his department to accompany SLED agent Tommy Robertson to interview David Lore of Connersville, Indiana. No one in Winnsboro knew who Lore was, but he was perhaps the single most important witness Young uncovered. Lore possessed the rifle that Beasley allegedly used to kill himself.

"In the summer of 1968 at the age of twelve, I was in Columbia with my family visiting my uncle, Richard Bane," Lore told the officers. "During the visit, I recall my father, Ellwood Lore, was given a .22 rifle by my uncle Richard. In a conversation in the basement, it was stated that the gun was used in a suicide by my aunt's brother. My uncle told my dad that my aunt didn't want the gun in the house and would he take it. It remained in our home in Connerville until my father's death in 1981. At that time, my mother gave the rifle to me."

For the first time, the police had possession of the murder weapon. It had been missing since 1967.

On June 3, Robertson and Byrd teamed up to solicit a statement from Mattie Caldwell, who had performed the household chores for Sandra after Ron suffered his stroke. She was eighteen at the time and worked in the house on Forest Hills Drive five days a week, averaging ten to twelve hours a day. Mattie was folding clothes in the backyard the day Beasley was shot.

"Sandra Beasley was acting very strange and nervous that morning," recalled Mattie. "All the kids had been sent away. She told me to go outside and fold the clothes, and I noticed that the television was turned up unusually loud and the radio was turned up loud, too.

"Sandra had shut all the doors and windows in the house even though it was a hot day. While I was out in the yard, I heard one shot. Sandra came to the door and stated that Ron had shot himself. I noticed that Sandra had blood on her shorts. That morning, prior to the shooting, Jerry Truesdale came by and had a conversation with Sandra.

"I do not believe Ron Beasley shot himself. I don't believe that he was physically or mentally capable of doing so. I had never seen him get out of bed or walk unassisted. I don't believe he was physically or mentally capable of committing suicide, either. I worked for Sandra only two times after Ron's death because I was afraid of her."

With each interview, Young was convinced he was accumulating enough vital testimony to reopen the case. He now felt it was time to confront Sandra, and once again Robertson and Byrd were assigned for the important interview. Sandra had been incarcerated as Frances Scott Truesdale for about a year when Robertson and Byrd arrived at the Virginia Women's Correctional Institute in Goochland on June 6. They talked for about two hours.

Frances's statements were completely opposite of what Robertson and Byrd heard from other witnesses. She claimed Ron Beasley had no use of his left arm, approximately 10 percent use of his left leg and 100 percent use of his right arm, no use of his right leg and drifting mental state.

She claimed that Beasley learned to control his urine and they planned his bowel movements, that he could carry on a conversation and could feed himself and she never once had to do so. She also stated that Ron could get out of bed and move around the house on his own, that he had days of depression but also had days when he was in a positive state of mind.

Finally, Frances admitted to becoming romantically involved with Jerry Truesdale. However, she said it happened approximately a month after Ron's death. She married Truesdale a few days later.

Young then directed a bold move. He wanted some dialogue from Jody Truesdale, Ron's only son, who was only a year old when his father died. If Jody would cooperate, a year after the Truesdale murder case and the only father he ever knew, by revealing facts that weren't brought out during the trial, Young would have compelling testimony with which to move and seek an indictment in the death of Ron Beasley.

Jody was cooperative. He revealed that his mother told him that she hoped they wouldn't reopen the case in Winnsboro because she didn't want the police to trouble his grandparents K.C. and Eva Beasley, who were now in poor health. Jody disclosed to the investigative officers that his mother kept a loaded .22 in her purse. He remembered her killing a dog with it one day. They were changing a tire on the side of the road, and right in front of all the children, Frances shot and killed the poor animal.

"I use the gun to keep the dogs away," Jody remembered his mother saying.

Jody was convinced his mother was a pathological liar, that he had been lied to all his life about everything. She told all of her children that she put $100,000 of insurance money from their father's death in a fund to help unemployed truck drivers. Jody was vocal about it and said it was all "bullshit."

What Frances did was take a $100,000 insurance check that was supposed to be split among the five sons and asked them to sign the money back to her. They did and never received a dollar.

The oldest son, Russell, had an even more exasperating awakening. He received a letter informing him that he would be getting disability checks. He never knew anything about the letter because Frances kept it from him. She then began intercepting and cashing the checks herself. Then one day, Russell got a letter informing him that he had to pay the money back.

Jody told them something else that was strange. At the funeral parlor, Frances asked everyone to leave so that she could spend ten minutes alone with her husband. He believes, now, that his mother might have buried the .22 in the casket with the remains of Jerry Truesdale.

Finally, Jody admitted that his mother was not a loving person, as portrayed during the trial, although she did cover for him and the other kids when necessary. However, she didn't express much affection toward them or his father. Now, he emphasized, none of the children believed that their mother was innocent. She never told them that she didn't do it, never told them face to face that she was innocent.

That's all Young had to hear. His instincts that Sandra killed Ron Beasley that he lived with for twenty-seven years were indeed true. Before filing for an indictment, he had to do one more thing. He wanted to exhume the body of his friend, and he needed K.C. Beasley's permission to do so. K.C. wasn't afraid of not seeing his grandson, Jody, anymore, which Sandra threatened him with since 1967. She was in jail, and Jody was a married man of twenty-nine. K.C. told Young to go ahead.

Herman Young couldn't ask for anything more. His thirty-year wait was nearing its end.

21

ANOTHER TRIAL

By the time the Republicans held their Grand Old Party convention in mid-August in San Diego, more rain had fallen on Johnny Porter's cotton crop than in all the previous two months. The old adage that if it rained on the first day of the month it would do so with regularity the remainder of the period held true. A record five inches watered his field and made Porter a believer in the centuries-old wives' adage. His crop was safe for picking now, sometime in the latter part of October, and he couldn't have been happier that the earth he plowed would yield its first crop of cotton in Fairfield County in fifty years.

Strom Thurmond would smile at that. A deep-rooted South Carolinian, he looked out for his constituents throughout the state from the first day he arrived in office in 1933. At ninety-three, Thurmond was attending his fifteenth national convention. He first appeared as a Democrat in the 1932 bash in Chicago, the year Franklin Delano Roosevelt was nominated as the party's standard-bearer. The venerable Thurmond almost upstaged the 1996 convention in San Diego, drawing crowds and ovations from admirers wherever he appeared. He belied his age, which would certainly be a campaign issue in November, by maintaining a busy schedule.

His regimen began each morning with thirty minutes of calisthenics. Over breakfast of skim milk, yogurt and granola cereal topped with fresh fruit, Thurmond perused the clippings from the state newspapers. Then he'd be off to morning meetings, a luncheon in his honor, private afternoon meetings, appear on the convention floor, an evening GOP gala of some sort and a midnight dinner-dance and cruise with the state delegation. That was just one day's effort.

On the convention floor nightly, Thurmond captured the audience. He was often mobbed by delegates, television crews and reporters from the print and electronic media. Thurmond warmed to the attention and made time for all of them.

"That man is a legend," exclaimed state GOP chairman Henry McMaster. "He's the most recognized person in the world."

And he possessed a sharp wit, too. One delegate, smiling broadly, greeted Thurmond with a big handshake.

"Senator," he began, "you won't remember this, but you kissed my wife forty years ago."

Thurmond didn't back off. "Bring her back and I'll kiss her again," he shot back without hesitation. The sharp-eyed senator also had a curt observation of a movie star. At one function, he was introduced to actor Charlton Heston. Later that evening, Thurmond remarked to his aide, "He looks so old, hardly recognized him."

It was no wonder why he was a media darling and why they followed his every move looking for such quick barbs and why hundreds of other well-wishers beseeched him for autographs and photos. From all appearances, he would be a difficult opponent to beat in his November reelection bid against Democrat Elliott Close. Thurmond in the national arena was, indeed, a man for all seasons.

Thurmond had visited Winnsboro a number of times and also campaigned there. Ed Arnette looked on him as a compassionate leader who truly cared about his constituents. He once helped Arnette acquire his postal route in Fairfield County when he was younger and raising four children. Uncle Ed knew a political power broker who knew Thurmond who in turn sent word to the county leader to see what he could do for him. By five o'clock one evening, Ed had his route.

On a more personal note, Arnette was indebted to the gregarious senator. His daughter, Fran, was a month short of graduating college and decided to continue her education at the Charleston School for Medicine. However, she needed a recommendation from a state official. Ed wrote a letter on her behalf to Thurmond and instructed Fran to mail the letter as quickly as possible.

Fran did better than that. Thurmond appeared on the Newberry campus for a speech, and she made it her mission to meet him. She succeeded and personally handed him the letter. The very next morning she received a phone call from Thurmond's secretary informing her that the senator would indeed dispatch his recommendation to the Charleston institution. After that, Ed Arnette became the biggest Thurmond fan in Winnsboro.

Porter's cotton was turning into a field of white. The much-needed late summer rain would save his crop. No one in Fairfield County had seen anything like it in fifty years, and the likable Porter was beaming in the early evening hour while looking across the expanse of his twenty-five acres. He had the look of the comic strip character Li'l Abner. Al Capp would have loved him.

The bountiful rain was enough to tease the parched earth as the leaves of the plants glistened and turned a deep green in color. Maybe there was something after all to the old wives' tale that if it rained the first day of the month, then the rest of the month would be wet. Porter had already harvested his wheat and sacked his one hundred acres of Silver Queen corn, and all that was left in the months ahead was some field corn and his first year of cotton.

But when he looked down for a closer look at his plants, he shook his head in disbelief. He had endured drought and the thrips, but now he discovered another enemy. A new blight was his nemesis now. He wondered what else could happen to his cotton.

"Isn't this something," he asked out loud. "I've got to get some pesticide and spray again or I'll lose the whole field for sure. Have to do it quickly, too."

Since it was Sunday, there wasn't anything he could do. Sleep didn't come easy that night. The next day, he learned that his problem was stranger than he imagined after waking with the feeling that all his hard labor would be wasted. He detected that it wasn't a blight that had invaded his crops but a chemical residue from an adjacent railroad track that hadn't been used for years.

The unused track belonged to the Fairfield County Railroad Museum, and Porter telephoned to find out what took place without his knowledge. He was told that Rufus Timms had sprayed the tracks earlier in the week. Continuing his pursuit, Porter then called Timms for the identity of the chemical compound's remnants that wafted from the track and ultimately landed on his cotton plants. Timms revealed that a portion of the spray was contaminated. The only consolation that Porter derived was that it affected only about an acre of his cotton, and after two days of apprehension both Porter and his cotton had survived the latest ordeal.

No one knew whether Sandra Beasley would survive the ordeal of another trial. Quietly, one weekend in early September, she was extradited from the Women's Correctional Institute in Goochland, Virginia, to the less accommodating Fairfield County Detention Center to await trial for the July 6, 1967 slaying of her husband, Ron Beasley.

She made it a point to tell the two deputies who accompanied her, SLED agent Tommy Robertson and Captain Robert Byrd of the Fairfield County Sheriff's Office, that she was a model prisoner in Goochland. She also asked if it were possible to see her friend—Sheriff Young.

22

OLDEST CASE

For two months, Frances Truesdale waited in the Fairfield County Detention Center for her trial to begin in the murder of her third husband, Ron Beasley. Unlike the Roanoke trial, Frances couldn't select her own attorney. She was broke, and being indigent meant that a public defender would be in charge of her fate. She could only hope that she would have one who believed in her ordeal that was declared a suicide thirty years ago.

If Frances was financially stable, she would have solicited a high-powered attorney out of Columbia, someone like Jack Swerling, who specialized in death penalty cases. His most recent one, in 1996, attracted attention throughout the state. Swerling represented Episcopal bishop William Beckham's son, Stephen, who was charged with the slaying of his wife, Vickie.

Vickie Beckham was the daughter of State Senator Jim Lander. The killing took place in Newberry County, some thirty-five miles west of Winnsboro. It wasn't a typical husband-wife murder. Rather, it was a classic murder-for-hire case. It was a tough case, and for something of that nature, it was worth a couple hundred thousand dollars to Swerling.

In the months before the murder, Beckham had spent quite a bit of time in Myrtle Beach, a popular seaside spot that is popularly called the Redneck Riviera. One of the town's most notable residents was mystery author Mickey Spillane who could have easily established the plot in one of his books. It was at this seaside oasis that Beckham formulated the idea to have his wife killed.

He contracted, not with a professional killer, but with Richard Anderson, of all people, a bouncer at a bar. However, the scheme didn't work to Beckham's expectations. Instead, Anderson turned state's evidence and fingered Beckham. Swerling didn't get Beckham acquitted. Rather, he got him life in prison instead of the death penalty and, for that, certainly earned his fee.

That was the quality of attorney that Frances needed for her Winnsboro trial. Instead, without money, she had no choice but to accept public defender Robert FitzSimmons as her legal counsel. Like Swerling, he was from Columbia, only far removed from all the support team that a prestigious law firm contains. FitzSimmons, who had been in law practice since 1986, was limited to an unattended office adjacent to the Fairfield County Courthouse. For his services, he received a monthly retainer as the county's only public defender and didn't earn an extra fee in murder cases. He received the same stipend every month whether he handled five cases or fifty.

FitzSimmons wasn't at all eager to defend Frances. He had never experienced a murder case quite like this one. Thirty years was a long time to argue over somebody's life. In fact, if he had a choice, he wouldn't have taken the case. But as the only public defender, he couldn't refuse the assignment, which he would have if he was in private practice.

FitzSimmons admitted privately that he "wasn't in a hurry to take it on because of the oddity of the case. I had no conflict of interest, so I had to take it."

It wasn't the first murder case that FitzSimmons had to defend. He represented several, but this was the first one ever in Fairfield County that took thirty years to reach the courts. Because of all the publicity the case generated nationally on two earlier television shows, as well as locally, he realized the difficulty he would encounter in defending Frances. His first desire was to ask for a change of venue simply because the interest in Winnsboro among the people who knew about the case was quite strong against his client.

There were a number of people he came in contact with at the courthouse who claimed they had always been convinced that she killed Ron Beasley. When he asked them to sign an affidavit so that he could get the venue changed to a county where the case wasn't so widely known, they refused. "They realized I was trying to help Frances and they didn't want that," concluded FitzSimmons.

None of the other murder cases he was associated with took as much of FitzSimmons's time as this one. In the others, there were three or four witnesses, including the cops and a pathologist. There was very little to be done because the cases were generally very hopeless—"open and shut" is the way that FitzSimmons described them. But this case was extremely different. It was not lost on FitzSimmons that it had occurred thirty years ago and that alone troubled him. What disturbed him even more was that the evidence had essentially disappeared, yet there were a number of witnesses involved. FitzSimmons had his work cut out for him, and he spent a month in preparation for Winnsboro's belated murder trial and a celebrated one at that.

Frances Truesdale was quite a contrast to FitzSimmons's other murder clients. Most of them weren't high school graduates, none was over thirty-five years old and none had stable jobs. Most were in their late teens or early twenties, "chronic ne'er-do-wells," is how FitzSimmons identified them.

Frances was indeed different in his eyes. FitzSimmons found her to be quite intelligent, capable of earning a college degree and a good conversationalist. He formulated the opinion that she was probably a handful when she was younger and very good looking, "a combination of sort of a bad girl, wild spirit and good looks," as he put it. He realized that Frances's past was not very good up to the time she married Jerry Truesdale. She had been married three times before she was twenty-five, had changed her name and briefly used someone else's identity.

"She was afraid," reasoned FitzSimmons, "afraid of her first husband. She was very young and finally realized it was stupid and foolish and changed her name back to make sure the proper names were on the children's birth certificates. When she had three children with her second husband, Bill Fitch, her maiden name was incorrectly listed and she wanted to fix that."

As a public defender for six years, FitzSimmons was quite familiar with the Fairfield County Courthouse, appearing there every time that court was in session. Designed by Robert Mills, a famous architect, and built in 1823, it is a stately and imposing two-story building in the middle of town rising majestically on Congress Street.

The classic building is a large, rectangular structure covered with a simple gabled roof that extends over the building in front and covers a broad flagstone portico. The four massive white columns supporting the portico are well proportioned and graceful. Originally, two flights of wooden steps led up to the second floor, but when the building was renovated and enlarged in 1939, the circular stairs of wrought iron and brass and a balcony were added. During the Civil War, the courthouse was ransacked and designated to be burned by Union troops. However, one of the high-ranking officers was a Mason, and when he observed the framed Masonic documents on the wall, he spared the place.

On November 18, 1996, Frances Truesdale, known as Sandra Beasley in Winnsboro, would take her place alongside Robert Mills as his courthouse's oldest case.

23

SANDRA BACK IN WINNSBORO

If it wasn't for Herman Young, the murder trial of Sandra Beasley would have never taken place in laid-back Winnsboro. The findings of the Virginia State Police, which were given to the previous administration of the Fairfield County Sheriff's Office, lay dormant in the files for two years, virtually ignored. The Virginia authorities had strongly recommended that they believed Sandra could have killed Ron Beasley from statements they received from witnesses in the Jerry Truesdale murder. Yet nothing was done until Young took office in 1993. He knew Ron didn't commit suicide but was murdered instead. Being elected sheriff gave him the opportunity to prove it.

He moved quickly to launch his investigation. He gave the assignment to a member of his staff, Captain Robert Byrd, a no-nonsense former serviceman who had distinguished himself in his twenty years on the force. Fortified with confidential files from the Virginia police, Byrd was joined by Lieutenant Tommy Robertson of the South Carolina Law Enforcement Division in Columbia gathering additional testimony for an indictment in the murder of Ron Beasley. After two years, the trial charging Sandra Beasley with murder made it to the court in the old mill town of Winnsboro.

Yet Young appeared a bit nervous. He had worried for years that after all the elapsed time witnesses might disappear or that Pop Beasley might die before the trial reached the courts. He also was concerned that too much publicity would create a delay or force the trial to be held in another county.

In a nascent setting in the old courthouse in the middle of downtown Winnsboro, replete with its ghostly past, Ann Letrick was seated, of all places, among some one hundred candidates of a jury pool when circuit court judge Don Rushing presided over the proceedings the morning of November 18, 1996. She sat there with a puckish smile in the very front row with a jury button pinned to the lapel of her blue suit, wondering how a thing like this could happen. Ann dutifully reported with her jury notice, fully realizing that she would be disqualified. It didn't matter. The euphoria of being there in an official capacity gave her a feeling of satisfaction and power. She sat tall and proudly for everyone to notice.

The aged courthouse, dating back to the Civil War, offered a somewhat warm and homey setting for the biggest criminal case in its existence. It was a beehive of excitement just before the doors opened. Both sides of the courtroom were filled. The jury pool was seated on the left and the spectators on the right. The eight chandeliers that hung from the high ceiling provided soft lighting to the oak-lined chamber, which comprised nine rows of wooden graduated seating, much like church pews in one of the town's many houses of worship. The ten tall windows adorned with Venetian blinds provided ample daylight to filter into the carpeted courtroom.

FitzSimmons was quite familiar with the Fairfield County Courthouse, appearing there every time that court was in session. The thirty-year-old case was officially recorded as *The State vs. Frances Sandra Beasley Truesdale*, which sounded like a name out of the social register of the Garden Club of Winnsboro. However, the cumbersome title didn't mean a thing to those in the courtroom. They all knew the defendant as Sandra Beasley.

After Ann was quickly and automatically disqualified, she smiled, took off her jury badge and moved to the right side of the room, where the spectators were seated. She sat directly behind Sandra next to her sister, Judy, who had driven from Milledgeville, Georgia. Both were neatly attired and looked confident.

Sandra appeared gaunt. She was smartly dressed in a black-and-white plaid jacket and a black skirt. Her gray hair was gathered in a ponytail and secured with a black ribbon. Her high cheekbones drew attention to a pale face. One could sense that she was a very attractive woman thirty years earlier. Symbolically, her fingers displayed two wedding bands, one on each hand.

Sitting in the front row, Ann Letrick was making a statement. She was the one who helped gather information from Sandra and gladly presented it to Special Investigator Barry Keesee of the Virginia State Police who investigated her brother's death for three years before the trial reached the courts in Roanoke, Virginia, in 1991. Keesee's compelling testimony was instrumental in helping the prosecution convict Sandra of second-degree murder in the killing of her fourth husband, Jerry Truesdale.

Keesee was present for the trial, which was expected to last about three days. However, he kept a low profile. He quietly remained out of view, preferring anonymity in the sanctuary of the sheriff's room located in the rear of the two-story courthouse. He was available if the state needed him to testify. The feeling among the prosecution was that they were confident with the witnesses they had summoned, and it was doubtful that Keesee would be asked to take the stand.

Frail and sickly, Red "Pop" Beasley was now eighty years old and wasn't expected at the trial. Emphysema had made it difficult for him to breathe. He was on the witness list, but no one anticipated his testimony. It would be too emotional for him to do so. All Pop Beasley was looking for after all these many years was closure for the death of his only son. He had lived without an ending for too long.

Judge Rushing was in complete control of his courtroom and left no margin for error. He spoke clearly with a firm southern accent and enunciated his words with conviction. Rushing made it understood that he was the law, much like a judge in an old western movie. Twice during the opening hour of the trial, he sternly admonished those who contaminated his courtroom with misconduct.

The first was a prospective juror who arrived fifteen minutes late after the scheduled nine o'clock hour. A short while later, the judge's dander was aroused for a second time when laughter broke out after 95 percent of the jury pool stood when asked if they owned a gun or if there was one in the immediate family. Rushing's face reddened with anger as he addressed the prospective jurors. Then he turned and pointed his finger at several members seated in the VIP box to his right. Rushing made no mistake that the courtroom was solely his domain and would be for as long as the trial continued.

The jury selection consumed most of the first day. It wasn't completed until after the lunch break. After Rushing gave the twelve jurors a zealous welcome, he dismissed them until the following morning. Once they left the courtroom, he asked the attorneys for motions.

The most relevant one was made by Robert FitzSimmons, the attorney for the defendant. He petitioned that the trial be conducted in another county, arguing that his client could not receive a fair trial in Winnsboro because of the publicity that had permeated the case for months leading to the trial. Rushing replied that he would take the motion into consideration and would render his decision the next morning.

After thirty years, the townsfolk got their first look at a woman they knew as Sandra Beasley. She looked quite different now, but it was her all right.

24

NO CHANGE OF VENUE

There was a decreased number of court goers when the second day of the trial resumed on a mild, overcast November morning. Most of the spectators consisted of the Beasley and Truesdale families, who sat together in a display of solidarity. One member on the Truesdale side was conspicuous by his presence. He wasn't in attendance the first day, but when Jody Truesdale entered the courtroom accompanied by his wife, it created a stir. They sat on the aisle behind the last row of family members. He was a father now himself, raising two daughters in Winston-Salem. Not once did Jody look toward his mother, who was now the defendant in killing his natural father, Ron Beasley, and she was only fifty feet in front of him. Although she never looked back, Sandra felt her son's presence in the courtroom.

The prosecution was seated on the left side of the room. Fairfield County solicitor, the appropriately named John Justice, would argue the state's case. He was joined by assistant solicitor J. Kim Roberts, Sheriff Young, Captain Byrd and local attorney Kenny Goode, who was instrumental in clearing Representative Tim Wilkes in the Lost Trust case that shook the state's political chambers in 1990. Wilkes owed Goode his political life.

Practically penniless, with almost every dollar gone from the $280,000 insurance money she received after Jerry Truesdale's death, Sandra's fate was strictly in the hands of a court-appointed public defender, Robert FitzSimmons. A Winnsboro attorney, James Barlow Loggins, was retained to aid FitzSimmons, and he made his presence felt during the jury selection the day before. Sandra, seated to the left of FitzSimmons, appeared confident.

Contrastingly, the two lead attorneys were courtrooms apart in appearance. Solicitor Justice, stern-faced, appeared in a rumpled suit that resembled a JC Penney purchase. FitzSimmons was a preppy type, someone out of *GQ* magazine. He wore a conservative but neat dark gray suit adorned by a red and blue tie and accented by a white handkerchief in his jacket pocket. He had a receding forehead with thick brown hair on the sides and back and resembled Mr. Chips, the storied British professor.

There were several theories that evolved in the Beasley murder that FitzSimmons pondered. The one that interested him most was that the actual killer could have been Jerry Truesdale, the Vietnam veteran who was no stranger to guns and killing and was passionately and openly in love with Sandra. Such an equation would have prevented a wife from testifying against her husband, and they were married twenty-nine days after Ron's death. What possibly might have developed twenty-one years later in 1988 was that the weight of consciousness reached a saturation point in that Truesdale decided he was going to tell all. Since Sandra would have been implicated as an accessory, she had no choice but to kill Jerry herself and remove the one person who knew how Ron was killed. Logistically, it was conceivable.

The other was that Ron Beasley could actually have walked through his house that July morning. FitzSimmons had a hospital report that read at the time of Ron's discharge from Fairfield Memorial Hospital, that "patient walked with the help of an orderly." This was a vital revelation for his defense, a key bit of documented information that could overcome all the state's witnesses who claimed that Beasley was paralyzed and couldn't walk. It was just possible that Ron summoned enough energy and strength to load a shotgun and, enraged by Sandra's indiscreet steamy affair with Truesdale in the very same house, shot at her first before turning the gun on himself.

After FitzSimmons met Sandra for the first time, he liked her. He didn't know much about her early childhood, but he was able to form an opinion about her background and was impressed with the way she conducted herself during the several conversations he had with her.

FitzSimmons had put in over a month's work on preparation for what he considered a difficult case. The file alone that solicitor John Justice presented him with was denser than most. FitzSimmons put in long hours to prevent being overwhelmed by the oldest case he or any other lawyer in the state ever had. The thirty years it remained open created a great deal of doubt and opinion, not evidence. He had more witnesses to examine, more papers and more incidents to research. The eight murder cases he had tried previously were cut and dried, a pathologist, three or four witnesses, including the police, and for the most part hopeless.

FitzSimmons carefully designed his strategy because of Sandra's conviction in the death of Jerry Truesdale. He believed she would make a convincing witness, but he also knew that he couldn't subject her to taking the witness stand and leaving her wide open for the prosecution to devour.

"I realized that we needed to make sure the jury was not aware of Sandra's conviction in the killing of Jerry Truesdale," explained FitzSimmons. "If they knew, they would immediately assume that if she killed him, she had also killed Beasley. In my closing statement to the jury, I intend to remind them that there were law enforcement officers operating thirty years ago. There were also a number of people who formed a judgment that this was a suicide, a coroner and investigating officers."

FitzSimmons was thinking ahead. He didn't expect the trial to consume more than three days, but on the final one, he wanted to make certain to be the last one to address the jury. "We had the advantage that if we didn't call any witnesses in being able to argue last," claimed FitzSimmons. "This is a tremendous advantage because when the jury goes to the jury room, the last lawyer they heard is the lawyer who has had the chance to answer the other lawyer's arguments and put things in their minds."

Before the jury was seated, Judge Don Rushing profoundly demonstrated, almost to the point of sounding liverish, that he was in complete charge of the courtroom, making it clear that if any of the attorneys challenged him, they had better be certain of their action. Rushing was determined that the trial would not evolve into a media circus like the O.J. Simpson charade. He allowed one television pool camera near the side of the jury but had it hidden behind a large slate blackboard. He then looked at the public defender and denied his previous day's motion in which he petitioned for a change of venue. The Beasley murder trial would be conducted in Winnsboro, and Rushing was unequivocally in charge of the proceedings. The trial was expected to last another two days and become a part of the state's history because of its unique nature with Rushing as the judge on record.

After the jury was ushered into the courtroom and seated, Rushing quickly explained the presence of the blackboard. The jurors represented a strange chemistry. Eleven of the twelve were Black and only three were women. None appeared to be professionals, except perhaps one or two. All of them turned their attention to the blackboard.

"Under our court rules, it is permitted to have what is called video coverage, television, radio coverage, newspaper coverage," pointed out Rushing. "The newspaper has always been in the courtrooms; they have not been permitted to use any photographic equipment. That is now allowed by our rules. Part of those rules provide that they cannot show or depict you, the jury. I have already made sure that doesn't occur.

"If there is any violation and I detect it, they are out of this courtroom and I am going to hold them in contempt of court and that cameraman will not be operating a camera for a while because I am going to put him in jail."

Rushing was firm. He then went on to explain the meaning of the word *solicitor*, informing them that it came from the English and that in most states these individuals were called district attorneys. Rushing further explained that the solicitors were elected by popular vote.

"What solicitor Justice tells you in his opening statement is not evidence," continued Rushing. "Remember that. It is not evidence. After he identifies to you what are the issues in this case, then the attorney for the accused person—we call a person who is accused of a crime a defendant—will speak. The defendant in this case is Frances Scott Truesdale, formerly known as Sandra Beasley.

"After the opening statements are completed, we then will move into the presentation of the evidence, and this is the phase of the trial that you, as a juror, are most concerned with because that is what you are here to judge, the evidence. You are not here to judge the lawyers or judge the judge or to judge anybody else but the evidence and those witnesses. The State brought this charge so they have the duty of proving what they say, and they must prove that by what we call proof beyond a reasonable doubt."

Rushing had the jury's attention. He spoke with authority and confidence. He explained that in a criminal trial, there were basically three categories of evidence. Rushing named them and explained sworn testimony, exhibits and stipulation of fact. The last required further explanation.

"That is exactly what it sounds like it would be, it is an agreement," commented Rushing. "This is where the attorney for the State and the attorney for the accused have agreed to some issue of fact that may have been in dispute and they no longer dispute it, so if they no longer dispute it, they can say, 'we agree to it.' And by agreeing to it, they don't have to put up a witness or offer an exhibit to prove it."

After identifying court procedure and legal terminology, Rushing explored the area of reasonable doubt. He repeated the phrase often enough in his opening remarks, and like a professor instructing a college law class, Rushing made certain his points were understood.

"The State must remove that presumption of innocence, and if they fail to do so, then it is under your oath and your duty to find that person not guilty," he emphasized. "You and I are called judges. I am the judge of the law. The jury is the judge of the facts. This is an important case to the State of South Carolina and this person, this accused person. Let's give them what everyone expects, our attention, our fairness, our impartiality.

"They've got to present evidence that you find to be truthful that meets the burden of proof, does it convince you beyond a reasonable doubt. That is what you do as a jury. You judge the facts. No one else can do that but you. If based on your consideration of the evidence you are firmly convinced that the defendant is guilty as charged, you must find her guilty. If, on the other hand, you think there is a real possibility that she is not guilty, you must give her the benefit of the doubt and find her not guilty. That is the burden of proof."

"All twelve of you must agree on the verdict. The State must prove beyond a reasonable doubt the taking of the life of the victim by this defendant, the killing, and that the time of the taking of that life that it was done with malice aforethought, either expressed or implied. I look forward to trying this case with you."

The first to deliver his opening statement was Justice. He cleared his throat and walked directly to the jury box. He started to pace up and down in short steps as he began his delivery. And he quickly seized on what Rushing had said earlier.

"I will concede from the very beginning that there is a unique quality to this case," admitted Justice. "The uniqueness does not lie in the evidence. The unique side of this case is that it occurred in July of 1967, over twenty-nine years ago. Any criminal trial is a step back in time, re-creating for a jury something that happened in the past. Quite often that past is six months ago or a year ago or two years ago. In this case it is much longer.

"I feel sure the defense will try to confuse the issue by saying in effect, 'Why weren't these charges brought then? Why wasn't she charged and tried in front of a jury in the sixties or the seventies?'"

Justice stopped briefly for a sip of water. He did so to make his point about time. He turned to the jury and continued, sounding like a high school history teacher.

"1967 was in fact a long time ago," acknowledged Justice. "Ladies and gentlemen, that is not the issue. Lyndon Johnson was president of the United States. John Kennedy had only been dead four years or less. Bobby

Kennedy and Martin Luther King were still living. The war in Vietnam had not reached its peak. *The Andy Griffith Show* was the number one TV show in the nation. The Beatles were riding high.

"I remember my status because I had just completed the bar exam the previous Friday and was not even a sworn lawyer yet. Mr. FitzSimmons, the defense attorney, was preparing to enter fourth grade in Columbia, ironically as it turned out, to be taught by the lady I would marry in the month of August, my wife.

"Many of us that are asked to recall what we were doing at a particular time in 1967 couldn't do it. But those people to whom Red Beasley was an integral part of their lives and who the violent death of Red Beasley was a traumatic moment in their lives, I submit to you their memories will be clear, their testimony will be detailed and convincing."

Once Justice returned to his seat, Rushing acknowledged FitzSimmons for his oration. FitzSimmons walked gingerly across the courtroom and stopped when he faced the jury. Cleverly, he scored an advantage in Justice's narration of time and outlining the events of twenty-nine years ago.

"As Mr. Justice said, this case is about something that happened a long time ago," began FitzSimmons. "I did start fourth grade that year and I enjoyed fourth grade, I enjoyed my teacher, but beyond remembering her name and where the building was, I don't have a very good memory of fourth grade. In twenty-nine years, evidence crumbles, people forget and some of the people who were there will die.

"This case is a sad story. This young couple, happy when they were married, were only married a short time when the husband had a stroke, what is called a berry aneurysm. It is a tiny little defect in his brain that had been there since he was born some twenty-five years earlier, that finally, like some seed long dormant, finally exploded, leaving Ronald 'Red' Beasley temporarily unconscious.

"The doctors diagnosed that he suffered hemiplegia, that is paralysis on one side up and down his body. Over time, Red began to use that side of his body as well as the undamaged side. This was a young man who was hospitalized in the prime of his life for six or seven weeks in Columbia, then he came back to Winnsboro and stayed in the hospital longer. His life changed dramatically. The happy stepfather of three and the father of a small baby was suddenly a man who had difficulty feeding himself and could not control his bowels. This man was not as happy as he had been.

"Unfortunately, he succumbed to the ninth most common cause of death in this country—he committed suicide. Since that time, myth and rumor have sprung up, stories have been told, half-truths have been spread around, various things have been said about Red Beasley and about his wife, Frances."

FitzSimmons wasn't concerned about history. Rather, if anything, he prepared himself well and began concluding his remarks.

"They are going to tell you about things that happened a long time ago," repeated FitzSimmons. "But it was not so long ago that people in Winnsboro didn't have telephones, it was not so long ago there was no hospital here, it was not so long ago there was no sheriff here, it was not so long ago there was no coroners.

"In fact, there was a hospital, people had telephones, there was a sheriff, there was a coroner and there was an investigation into the death of Ronald Beasley. There are records of that investigation. And those records show stare decisis, 'it has been decided; it is so' that Ronald Beasley killed himself, died at his own hand."

Fred Robinson, the State's first witness, was weak. He was one of the investigating officers in the Beasley death, yet experienced trouble in recalling the events of the day. In his opening statement to the jury, just minutes before, FitzSimmons emphasized that people forget things that happened long ago, and Robinson proved him correct.

"How long did you stay as deputy sheriff?" asked Justice. "I can't remember the number of years," replied Robinson.

"After the detention center I believe you in fact were elected sheriff yourself, were you not? And that was 1976?"

"I think it was. No, I think it was '74."

"Now, I want you to think back Mr. Robinson. I realize it has been a long time ago, to July 6 of that year, 1967. Did you have an occasion along with an officer Brown to go to a location on Forest Hills Drive outside of the town of Winnsboro?"

"If my memory serves me correct, there were four of us. We were dispatched to a house, I believe it is going down towards Forest Hills, and the road goes from there all the way to what I think we used to call Possum Holler. If my memory is correct it was given to us there may have been a shooting or somebody was shot."

"Do you remember whether or not the person that was shot was still in the house or had he been removed to the hospital?"

"I'm not sure whether the body or the person was still there or if it had been taken to the hospital."

"Do you remember talking to the wife of the victim, which is Ms. Sandra Beasley?"

"I don't remember whether I talked with her or not."

FitzSimmons was pleased with what he heard when it was time for him to cross-examine the witness. Robinson's memory lapses were exactly what he strongly emphasized to the jury about remembering what happened twenty-nine years ago. Robinson couldn't even recall if Ron Beasley was lying on the floor of the house when he arrived to investigate a shooting. Surely one could remember looking at a body, certainly one of the traumatic moments that Justice alluded to in his opening monologue.

FitzSimmons continued to evoke Robinson's poor memory. He recognized an advantage.

"Do you recall having written down anything about this case?"

"No, sir, I do not."

"Would you and Chief Investigator Jack Robinson have discussed the case and pool[ed] your resources?"

"We probably would have if it would have been of a nature other than what was ruled on. Then I kind of put it in the back of my head. Over the years I hadn't heard anything else until just recently."

"And you have no recollection of any such discussion?"

"I don't have any recollection of that."

Funeral director Julius Cameron took the stand next. He had been associated with Pope Funeral Home for as long as anyone could remember and was a friend of Ron Beasley. One of the services of the funeral home was to provide ambulatory duties for the county.

"Do you recall the condition Mr. Beasley was in after late March of 1967?" inquired Justice.

"I remember that he had a subarachnoid hemorrhage, which is a stroke," answered Cameron.

"We had done ambulance work for him. Transporting him to and from hospitals at various times and I knew him to be virtually paralyzed from that stroke."

"Did you ever see him able to move from one place to another unassisted?"

"No, sir."

"Let me jump forward, if I can to July 6 of 1967. What was the situation as you remember it upon arrival at the Beasley home?"

"We had been called to go to the residence, that there had been a shooting."

"When you arrived there, where was Mr. Beasley?"

"As well as I remember, he was lying on the sofa in the living room."

"On the sofa?" asked Justice in surprise.

"It was either on the sofa or on the floor. I'm wanting to think it was on the sofa."

"I want you to think back a week earlier on July 1 of 1967. Did you have an occasion on that day to respond to a call to the Beasley home?"

"Transported him from his home to the hospital where he received lacerations with some type of knife or razor or razor blade."

"Do you recall whether he was conscious at that time?"

"No, sir."

"You don't recall?"

"To my knowledge he was comatose, I would say."

"In September of 1994, at the direction of Coroner Joe Silvia, did you perform another service involving the late Red Beasley?"

"Yes. The funeral home that I work for was contracted by the Fairfield County Coroner's Office to disinter the remains of Ronald Beasley, so that they could be transported to the pathologist in Newberry for autopsy examination of the remains."

The medical words used by Cameron bothered FitzSimmons. He didn't hesitate in diluting them when he began his cross-examination.

"Mr. Cameron, most of your medical knowledge is the product of years of observation and experience, isn't it?" posed FitzSimmons.

"Yes, sir."

"And your formal medical training is fairly slack?"

"I have no medical training other than simple first aid."

Having made his point, FitzSimmons then reverted to another line of questioning. He was determined to show the jury Beasley's mental state prior to his death.

"Isn't it fair to say that the Red Beasley that you saw when you carried him to and from the hospital was in considerably worsened condition and deteriorated from the Red Beasley that you had known in 1966?" pressed FitzSimmons.

"Yes, sir."

"Was he awake any time you saw him?"

"He was conscious but in a comatose state."

"Were you able to observe his apprehension, that is, his viewing of his surroundings?"

"I'm not sure that he would have been conscious of it."

"You are not sure?"

"That's right."

"Did you ever visit Red at his house?"

"No."

"During the time of his convalescence?"

"I did not."

The state's first two witnesses weren't very convincing. Justice tried to save the credibility of Cameron in his redirect: "One further question, did anybody in law enforcement ask you any of these questions in 1967?"

"No."

FitzSimmons got the final word in his re-cross: "Mr. Cameron, if you had any suspicion of any wrongdoing of any sort, would you hesitate to contact law enforcement, then or now?"

"No."

Helen Edwards, the director of medical records at Fairfield Memorial Hospital, followed Cameron on the stand. She had a file of records at her disposal, which resulted in some confusion that necessitated an interruption in the proceedings, which Rushing didn't appreciate, as copies of several pages needed to be made. A short while later, Justice continued with his questioning.

"Ms. Edwards, would you please under 'brief history,' would you read the first line as it was apparently originally written before the crossouts?"

"Laceration of left side of neck and left wrist with razor blade."

"What kind of change has been made in that sentence as it exists today?"

"The left wrist has been changed to right."

In re-questioning the witness, FitzSimmons further stressed the point.

"Ms. Edwards, in at least one point in those records the indication is left and then above in parentheses it says right; isn't that correct?"

"Yes, sir."

"That is in addition to the place where one has been crossed out and the other has been written in, isn't it?"

"Yes, sir."

"So, there are two places where which wrist was cut is indicated each way; isn't that correct?"

"Yes, sir."

At this point, Rushing ordered a recess, which he indicated would last about twenty-nine minutes while the attorneys straightened out the copy of the documents furnished by Ms. Edwards. It didn't appear to be a particularly good morning for the prosecution. But one of its star witnesses, Betty Ruth Truesdale McGinnis, would be the first to be summoned after the recess as Justice prepared to recover from a weak showing.

McGinnis had moved into the Beasley house the day after Ron suffered his stroke. She was sixteen at the time and already separated from her husband, Ben Branham. She was also Jerry Truesdale's cousin and afraid of Sandra in the months while she was waiting to testify.

25

SHERIFF YOUNG'S SURPRISE MOVE

Betty Ruth appeared frumpy and timid when she was summoned to the witness stand and wasn't looking forward to testifying. It was obvious within the first few minutes as she spoke in low tones. Twice she was asked to speak louder, first by Justice and a short while later by Judge Rushing himself.

"Please tell the jury what your relationship was with the Beasleys," posed Justice.

"I was a neighbor of theirs and friend and had, you know, visited with them," she answered weakly.

"Do you recall the situation I believe in late March, early April maybe of 1967 when Red Beasley had what we will call a stroke, did your relationship or your residence change in regard to the Beasleys?"

"Yes. At that time, a friend and I, Cookie and I were living in a trailer, and I was not married at the time. I had just separated, we did not have jobs, and we did babysit for Sandra and she helped us with the rent. When he had the aneurysm, she came to our residence that morning and we went and moved into her house to take care of the house and the children while Red was in the hospital."

"The lady you refer to as Cookie, would that be Alpha Chappell, now Alpha Chappell Tillman?"

"Yes."

"So basically, you lived in the Beasley household to look after the children in lieu of paying rent?"

"Yes."

"After Red Beasley came home from the hospital, what was his situation as you observed it?"

"Red Beasley was completely paralyzed on the right side. He had very, very little use of his left hand. He was incontinent. He had to be moved from place to place and could not walk on his own. He had the mentality of a child. He was very sweet, very trusting and very dependent on care."

Betty Ruth then acknowledged that she had drawn a sketch of the house when asked to do so by one of the investigators. Justice introduced a large board with the sketch blown up and labeled it State Exhibit 2. At that point, FitzSimmons raised an objection. His basis was that Justice had not laid an adequate foundation, arguing that the sketch as originally presented did not accurately reflect.

"Your honor, this is not a drawing she made," reasoned FitzSimmons. "It is not a drawing prepared in any sort of mathematical for close proportion to the drawing that she made."

FitzSimmons had a valid observation. The enlarged drawing gave the Beasley house an enormous look instead of the house it actually was. It was nowhere near what the drawing represented. The distorted look could give the jury a picture in their minds of such a large house that Beasley could never walk around by himself. Rushing pondered the objection for a moment and gave his opinion.

"I will let him use it demonstratively," ruled Rushing.

"I would prefer that," agreed FitzSimmons, "if he wishes to use it as a diagram, but as evidence is another story."

Betty Ruth was asked to step down from the witness stand and walk over to the board. When she answered the next question, Judge Rushing once again encouraged her to speak louder. She was uncomfortable in her role as a witness.

"Where did Mrs. Beasley sleep?" inquired Justice while pointing to the board.

"There was an extra bed in the front bedroom," pointed out Betty Ruth.

"With the children."

"Uh-huh."

"And where did you sleep?"

"On the couch in the living room."

Having established her presence in the house, Justice then asked Betty Ruth to describe Ron's condition in more detail. She added that he couldn't take care of himself and had very little use of his left hand. She repeated that he was incontinent and wet the bed a lot, which necessitated the use of linen savers or some type of diaper and that Ron could not carry on a conversation and had the mentality of a child.

"Was he able to feed himself with his left hand?" asked Justice.

"No, he wasn't. The only time that he used that, if you cut a sandwich in small pieces and placed it in his hand, he could put it up to his mouth. But we had to feed him something, to drink out of a cup with a straw and hold it for him. He would drool down the side of his mouth and we would have to wipe that."

Justice then got Betty Ruth to describe Ron's bedroom, where she said he spent most of his time. She also added that when he was moved to another room in the house, he had to be carried, sometimes by two people, and she never once saw him move from one room to another by himself.

"I noticed you mentioned the name Betty Ruth Truesdale McGinnis. Were you related to Jerry Truesdale?"

"I am. I am Jerry Truesdale's cousin, uh-huh."

"Was Mr. Truesdale ever in the home during June and early July of 1967?"

"Yes, he was."

"What was the relationship between he and Sandra Beasley as observed by you?"

"Very close relationship."

Justice asked Betty Ruth to describe what took place the morning of July 1. She complied without hesitation.

"I was awakened that morning and I heard Red moaning from his bedroom," began Betty Ruth. "I got up to see what was wrong with him. Before I got into the bedroom, Sandra cut me off and kept me from going in and told me not to go in there, that he tried to commit suicide. So, I went back out. Then she called for help. After he was taken away, I went in the bedroom and the bed was saturated with blood. He was supposed to have cut his wrist and throat."

"Now think back to the morning of the sixth of July. What do you recall about your movements and activities that morning?"

"I remember being in the home and Sandra being very insistent about me taking one of the little boys and going to the store. I remember it because I was busy doing something else and wanted to finish that before I left. She was very insistent that I go. So, I took the little boy and went in the truck and went to the store. I don't remember which store I went to, I think it was a grocery store. After that I stopped by my daddy's house. When I pulled up in the driveway somebody stopped and said, 'Did you know Red had killed himself.' I thought he was referring to the week before with the wrist cutting.

I said, 'No he didn't. I just left their house a little bit ago. He was fine.' When I got back to the house, he was already gone, and I found out that he supposedly shot himself."

"Red Beasley? Do you remember any firearms anywhere else in the house?"

"Other than Sandra always carried a handgun in her pocketbook."

"When you left taking the child with you to the store, where was he? Was he in the recliner in the living room?"

"Do you know how he got to that chair that morning?"

"I don't remember, no."

"After Red Beasley's death, did the relationship between Sandra and Mr. Truesdale take any changes in the immediate future?"

"After his death they remained very close, and they were married shortly after that."

FitzSimmons looked at his notes before he got up to cross-examine the witness. He didn't waste any time in working the memory angle, which he maintained was a relevant part of his defense.

"Where was Jerry Truesdale in March of 1967?" he challenged Betty Ruth.

"I'm not sure. I believe he may have been in Vietnam, sometime."

"Do you remember when he came home from Vietnam?"

"I remember him coming back to see me because we were related, but I do not remember the exact month."

"Could it have been as late as June 20?"

"I'm not sure."

"Do you have any idea when he came back?"

"No, I don't."

"Was it before or after Red had his stroke?"

"I think it was afterwards."

"Do you remember whether Red was present when he came home— when Jerry came by to visit you?"

"I'm not sure."

"You testified that Red could put pieces of a sandwich into his own mouth. Is that correct?"

"After they were placed cut into small pieces and placed into his hand, his left hand."

"But he could in fact move his hand?"

"Yes."

"Do you remember when he was in the hospital when he walked one night with the orderly's help?"

"No, I don't."

"Would it surprise you that there is a hospital record that he walked one night in May with the help of an orderly?"

"I didn't know about it."

In his redirect, Justice performed damage control. Betty Ruth not remembering so many things didn't sit well with him and, he sensed, with the jury. He reestablished her memory loss with a single question. He asked Betty Ruth if Sandra had told her how Red had died.

"She told me that he got up and went into the washroom and got bullets out of a box that were on a shelf. He then went back and got the rifle and loaded it and fired and shot himself."

The state's next key witness was Mattie Caldwell, a Black domestic who cleaned house and did the laundry. She had finished high school that summer and was the only one in proximity of the Beasley house when he was shot. In fact, she heard the shot while she was in the yard doing the laundry.

"Tell us what your observations were in regard to Mr. Beasley's condition after he came home from the hospital?" asked Justice, establishing continuity after Betty Ruth's testimony.

"Most of the time he was in bed, or sometimes I would get there and he would already be in the recliner chair."

"Did you ever see him walk just by leaning on a cane or anything of that nature?"

"No, I didn't."

"When he was moved from one place to another, how did that happen?"

"He was moved, someone moved him."

"How did Mr. Beasley eat?"

"He never did too much eating when I was there. A few times I fixed a sandwich and cut it in pieces and put it in his hand. I would always have a small cup of milk with a straw in it and I would put it to his mouth. But it was very little times that I did feed him."

"When you came to work on the sixth who was in the house?"

"Sandra and Red was in the house."

"Was Ms.—then Ms. Truesdale—Ms. McGinnis who just testified, was she in the house when you got there?"

"No. After she picked me up, she dropped me off and she left. I went on in the house from the back door."

"Where was Mr. Beasley when you saw him that morning?"

"He was sitting in the recliner chair."

"After you vacuumed the living room, what happened next?"

"She told me to save the kitchen for last and go outside and get the clothes off the line and fold the clothes at the clothesline."

"Is that the way you normally do it?"

"No. I usually bring them in the house and fold them."

"Has she ever told you to do that before?"

"No."

Mattie went on the explain that when she went out to fold the clothes, the television was on somewhat loud and that a radio resting on the kitchen window was also playing quite loudly.

"Approximately how long did you stay out at the clothesline?"

"I was folding clothes maybe three or four minutes I'm guessing, and as I was folding clothes [I] recall hearing a shot."

"Did you know at the time it was a shot?"

"Yeah. It sounded like a gun, and I thought it was some boys down the street shooting."

"After you heard the shot, what happened?"

"She came running to the back door and she said, 'Mattie, come inside.'"

"When you got inside, what was the situation?"

"I found Ronald lying face down on the floor with a rifle laying on the floor on the left side of him."

Rushing unexpectedly interrupted. The condition of a juror displeased him. "Madam juror," he remarked, "would you like some water? You look like you have a problem staying awake. Are you okay? You keep looking like you are dozing on me. Let me know if something is wrong, okay?"

Rushing didn't let anything get by in his courtroom, and Justice continued his questioning.

"What instructions did Sandra give you?"

"After I came in, I went straight where his body were and I knelt down on the floor. When I was getting up, she was on the telephone. I asked her who she was trying to call and she said she was trying to call his mother. So, I called his mother and I told Mrs. Beasley to get over here right away. I didn't tell her what happened."

"Where in the room was the blood you mopped up?"

"It was in front of the gun rack and the bookshelf."

"It wasn't where Red was lying?"

"No, it wasn't no blood where he was lying."

"Did you notice any blood on or about Sandra Beasley?"

"Yes. When she came to the back door, I noticed blood was on her shorts."

"Did you know Jerry Truesdale?"

"I seen him like stop by or something."

"Did you ever see him in the Beasley home?"

"No."

"Did you ever see him stop by outside the Beasley home?"

"Yes. I saw him the morning of Ronald's death."

"And who did he talk to?"

"I was cleaning the back bedroom and he pulled up in the back. She went out to see what he wanted and then he left. He never did come inside."

FitzSimmons softly approached Mattie. She was a kindly looking woman, a maternal type, and FitzSimmons didn't want to upset her in any way. Certainly not intimidate her. He was observant of her genteel manner.

"Did you enjoy being around him after his stroke?"

"Yes. He would motion when I walked into the room where he was. He would sort of smile at me and I would sit down and he would be watching TV. But he never said anything."

"He never communicated with you in any way?"

"No. He have said something I couldn't understand."

"But he would try to speak to you?"

"Yes. He would try to say something."

FitzSimmons didn't keep Mattie long. When he finished, Justice approached the bench: "Your Honor, with the court's indulgence, our next witness is here now, but I need about five minutes to talk with him. I can conclude with him before the lunch hour, if I can get a quick, short recess, no more than five minutes. It is Dr. Sexton."

Rushing affirmed his control: "All right solicitor, please do it promptly because the lunch time is 1:00," he ordered.

Dr. Sexton was a specialist in the area of pathology with subspecialization in forensic pathology in Newberry, South Carolina. After the brief recess, he explained that he performed an autopsy on the exhumed remains of Ron Beasley in 1994. He had performed about one hundred exhumations, but never one like this, he confessed. Ron's body was totally skeletonized.

He revealed that the only significant injury found to the skeletal portion of the body that was an acute injury was a gunshot wound. He explained that there was a hole in the base of the skull that corresponded to being inside the mouth and there was a bullet that was just inside the top of the skull near the back of the head.

Dr. Sexton further established the position of the bullet that killed Ron. He was able to put a probe through the hole in the base of the mouth and X-ray the position of the probe to show that when the bullet came to rest in the back of the head it came through the inside of the mouth. He indicated that the person had been shot by a gun placed inside the mouth or with the mouth open at the time the gun was fired.

He also disclosed that the bullet was consistent with the size of a .22 caliber, but oxidation would make it impossible to match it to a particular weapon.

"I was not able to say whether it was a .22 rifle or .22 pistol," conceded Dr. Sexton when he was asked by FitzSimmons.

After the lunch break, court reconvened at 2:30 p.m., and Justice was rapidly moving forward. He got SLED Agent Tommy Robertson to testify without the jury present about his interview with Sandra while she was still incarcerated in Goochland, Virginia, for Jerry Truesdale's murder. Robertson's answers the fifteen minutes he was on the stand were well documented and only required a minute of cross-examination by FitzSimmons.

Rushing then reviewed the legalities of the interview conducted by Robertson and Captain Byrd along with a witness. He cited two cases, *Jackson v. Denno* and *Miranda v. Arizona* in validating the interview, which was not given under duress or threat and ruled Sandra's statements admissible. He then told Robertson to step down and directed his next question at Justice.

"I understand they are going to call another witness?" Justice concurred.

"Solicitor, would you give us some guidance about your need for the rest of the panel?"

"Your Honor, I will either conclude my case today or within an hour of the morning hour," announced Justice.

Dr. William Bridgers, who was now eighty and attended Ron at the time of his stroke, brought several notes with him when he took the stand as the state's next witness. He described that Ron was unconscious in the emergency room when he saw him for the first time and observed that he was paralyzed on the right side but that he moved his left arm and leg with painful stimuli. When he regained consciousness several days later, he moved his left arm and leg on occasion.

Bridgers's notes and that of others on the hospital report were vital to FitzSimmons. He didn't hesitate in referring to them and rather than read them out loud himself, he asked Dr. Bridgers to read them clearly with the thought that it would be more effective from a medical standpoint. Bridgers spoke in low, soft tones and was barely audible.

"It was obvious that the patient had a right hemiplegia. He did not move his right arm except when it was pinched. He used his left arm frequently with scratching and the left arm was rather restive to movement whereas the right arm was relaxed. Both legs moved with painful stimuli but the right movement much less than the left. Patient voluntarily moved his left leg on occasions."

A few minutes later, FitzSimmons had Dr. Bridgers read aloud a notation made by Dr. Dubose: "At the time of discharge the patient was eating an adequate diet, was getting up in the chair with help, but was still incontinent of his bowels and still had a catheter in place."

Sandra had to be pleased with what she heard. FitzSimmons adeptly handled the medical part of the trial, and a doctor's admission that Ron had moved his legs and could get out of a chair with help, surely must have left an impression on the jury.

James Rutland, a next-door neighbor who last saw Ron alive on June 30, appeared for the state. He had brought Ron a bowl of oyster stew that his wife had made between five and six o'clock Friday evening before leaving for summer army camp the next morning. He claimed that Sandra fed Ron the stew and remembered Ron had drooled on the right side of his mouth.

"He was always drooling on the right side and some of the stew came down, and we sponged it off with a paper towel or either a napkin," said Rutland.

He didn't learn of Ron's attempted suicide until he called home from Fort Stewart the end of the following week. When he returned to Winnsboro on July 6, he was told that Ron shot himself. Rutland couldn't believe he had done so. Frustrated, he went to Sheriff S.L. Montgomery and asked why there wasn't any investigation.

Winnsboro attorney Kenneth Goode was the last witness of the day, and he knew Ron Beasley very well. Goode looked every part of an attorney with a pressed suit and a bow tie, which was his trademark. He appeared anxious to take the stand.

"Red was kind of a hero of mine," he began. "He was my Boy Scout Explorer troop leader. He also was real interested in automobiles. He had a drag car and a Hemi Plymouth that he would take me for rides in. And he would make me feel like a big shot because he would let me work on his cars with him. He was just a great guy and he spent a lot of time with me and the other scouts through the years."

Goode related how he visited Ron after his stroke and then on several occasions took him for a ride in his car, hoping it would be therapeutic. Goode noticed a look in Ron's eyes then as if he was going to try to speak. But all he did was make a sound, and Goode never could understand what his friend was trying to say.

"Was he able to walk?" asked Justice. Goode adamantly answered in the negative: "His condition was that he had no use of the right, period, exclamation point."

Goode remained imperious when he was cross-examined by the defense, and FitzSimmons, recognizing the big brother relationship of the two, didn't waste time keeping him on the stand.

"Did you ever see Red Beasley feed himself?" Goode appeared angry with the question.

"I've been listening to that same question being asked. I have seen Red being fed, but no, I have never seen Red feed himself."

After Goode stepped down, Justice informed the court that he would have at least one and no more than three witnesses for the next day's session and the state would rest its case. No one knew that one of the witnesses would be Pop Beasley. He summoned enough strength from Young's impassioned plea to appear. Unknown to anyone except the solicitor, it was Young who would secretly deliver Pop through the back door of the old courthouse on Main Street.

26

POP BEASLEY

At 9:30 on Wednesday morning, the opening of the trial was briefly delayed. Justice had requested a few additional minutes, and when they had elapsed, Rushing asked if the witness was now available. As he had demonstrated the first two days, Rushing's mien dominated the courtroom as he conducted his trial, which he knew would be written into the South Carolina law books as a point of reference because of its unique nature.

"The witness is here now," reported the solicitor, "and he will be my second witness."

The first was Joe Silvia, who had been the Fairfield County Coroner for twenty years in an elective capacity. He was also a full-time employee of the Manhattan Shirt Company and found time to work part-time at Pope Funeral Home. He confirmed that when he took office twenty years earlier, records that were kept before that time were turned over to him by his predecessor. Justice then asked him to explain for the jury's benefit the meaning of the word *inquest*.

"An inquest is held by the coroners around the state to determine if there is enough probable evidence to hold a person for grand jury action on any case that he might be faced with," elucidated Silvia.

"Would you read the entry under the death of Ron Beasley, dated June 6—or July 6, rather?" stumbled Justice.

"It says, 'The State versus the dead body of Ronald Keith Beasley, white male, age 28 years, lived at Forest Hills, Route 4, Box 70-B, Winnsboro,

South Carolina.' Mr. Boulware writes that 'On July 6, 1967, I viewed the dead body of the above deceased at the emergency room at Fairfield County Hospital. A bullet had entered his mouth which caused death. He had stitches in the left of his throat and left wrist which appeared to be recently done. Officers Fred Robinson and Brown investigated the incident and found two empty cartridges and said the rifle was laying by his side when they arrived. No inquest demanded and no inquest held. Death caused by self-inflicted wound.'"

FitzSimmons didn't move to cross-examine but was stunned when Justice called his next witness.

"The State calls Mr. Kirven Beasley," Justice loudly announced, almost with a look of pleasure on his stoic face. "Court's indulgence, your Honor, he is out in the back hall."

The spectators looked astonished as Pop Beasley slowly made his way into the courtroom from the same back door that Sandra used every day. Arthritis had claimed most of his body, and he exhibited trouble breathing. As Pop reached the witness stand, he appeared languid and pale. He gathered all his strength to appear in court. He wanted to go on record for the only son he ever had. Pop Beasley was known as "Big Red," but he lived without "Little Red" for thirty years, and the memory of his son's death haunted him to a degree that he became nervous when talking about him.

"Please tell us about Little Red after he returned home from the hospital after his stroke," requested Justice slowly.

"He was more or less helpless. He couldn't do for himself. He couldn't walk. He couldn't talk intelligently. He mumbled a little bit, but he couldn't talk. And he couldn't care for himself at all."

"Did you ever hear Sandra say anything about caring for him?"

"Two or three days before, I can't remember, she did make the remark to my wife and I overheard her in our driveway at home. She wasn't going to clean up that mess after him the rest of her life. She didn't intend to do that."

"Were you satisfied with the ruling?"

"No, I wasn't."

"Did you discuss it with law enforcement officials?"

"I didn't. I had a son-in-law that was a detective with the City of Columbia Police and I was more or less in shock. He went up and talked with the law enforcement and obtained the rifle that they had confiscated at the time. He told me that he asked them if they were going to take out a warrant for her. He said the sheriff made a remark to him that the coroner had ruled it a suicide, and as far as he was concerned that is what it was, suicide."

"Why did you not take out a warrant?"

"I felt if I had taken out a warrant that we would have just lost contact with my grandson. We had got fond of the baby and having it most of the time."

FitzSimmons didn't press Pop Beasley in his cross-examination. He had to repeat several questions because Pop, frail and thin with poor eyesight, was also hard of hearing. Pop couldn't recall if he helped with the funeral arrangement for his son with Julius Cameron. He was shown the funeral information sheet.

"I wouldn't have given this sudden suicide but the rest of it seems to be accurate," he remarked.

Justice's final witness was Herman Young. Like a chess player, he saved his best move for last. He knew Young would play well with the jury. Young was a handsome Black man, sharply dressed and articulate. Besides, he recently was reelected sheriff by a wide margin, 3–1, a popular figure around town. Justice didn't waste time in establishing the friendship Young had with Ron Beasley.

Young told him he was impressed with Beasley from the first day he met him at work at the UniRoyal plant.

"Red was very talented. He could weld aluminum. He also was one of the first welders that I knew that could weld upside down. I was very impressed with him when I first started working there and right away, he and I became fast friends."

"Did you become friends also with his parents?"

"Yes. Red and I always looked at each other as being brothers. I would quite often visit Mr. and Mrs. Beasley and they looked upon me as their son."

Young then related that he visited his friend quite often in the hospital and at home after his stroke.

"Almost every day. The hurting thing, Red was so active and so talented, and to see him in the condition that he was not able to do anything for himself. He was not able to speak. He was like a newborn, and when you talk to a newborn, you can't wait for that newborn to say the first word. I was so close with Red I wanted to just talk to him and wait for him to say something to me, 'Hey, buddy,' or something like that, but he never did. I would hold his hand and he could not even give you a squeeze or anything. It just wasn't there. I was hoping that he was trying to tell me something but I never heard a word."

Young had the attention of the court with his touching remembrance of his friend, and it left a few spectators weepy. Justice continued with his star witness.

"After the funeral, did you go by the home to further pay your respects?"

"I wanted to go by and just tell Sandra that even though Red was no longer with us, that I would be there for her for any chores. I just wanted to let her know that she had the support."

"Did you ever have that conversation?"

"No. When I left and got to the yard, and I had the windows down because it was a hot day, I could hear music and laughter inside the house. I just could not believe that such a short time after the funeral hearing such goings-on in the house."

"You didn't go in?"

"No, sir. I just sat and cried."

FitzSimmons didn't want any part of Young after his sobering testimony. Sandra looked directly at Young while he was on the stand, trying to make eye contact. Young never looked in her direction. And he didn't when he stepped down and returned to his seat as Justice rose and announced, "That is the case for the State of South Carolina, your Honor."

After the jury and the defendant was removed from the courtroom, Rushing asked for motions. FitzSimmons was the first to speak: "Your Honor, the first motion would be for a directed verdict. I do not believe that the State has proven beyond a reasonable doubt that they have proven that my client committed the crime she is charged with."

Justice was requested to answer: "The State feels we proved a circumstantial evidence case. It meets all the tests of circumstantial evidence. We put forth at least ten witnesses, both medical and lay witnesses, all of whom testified as to the inability of the deceased to have done anything for himself, leaving one and only one reasonable hypothesis—and that is that the defendant did indeed shoot and kill Mr. Beasley."

FitzSimmons asked to be heard briefly in reply: "As the court is aware, the standard when all of the evidence is circumstantial is that there must be substantial evidence. I do not believe Mr. Justice has supplied any substantial evidence. There has been no direct evidence that would show that my client killed her husband."

Rushing had to make a ruling on the defense's motion for a directed verdict. He didn't vacillate for a moment but instead quickly approached the issue without temerity. Rushing summed up his decision without equivocation: "The deceased was a person who had become an invalid, helpless in his condition, who had suffered a severe stroke. By the substantial medical testimony in this case and by other witnesses, that he was unable to perform any bodily functions without assistance. He was incontinent;

he could not feed himself; he had at the very least very limited use of any remaining hand or arm.

"The doctor's testimony in that regard and the other witnesses seemed to clearly indicate to this court that it would be highly impossible, if not improbable, that he could exercise the events for which were accounted to as to the basis of his death, that he could move himself, take bullets, load a gun, take the weapon and then fire shots. The court therefore denies the motion for a directed verdict."

Rebuffed, FitzSimmons kept trying. He tried a different approach: "Your Honor, I request the court to allow us to argue further on the earlier motion for dismissal on the grounds of due process."

Rushing gave him the opportunity. FitzSimmons began his rationale.

"The State's case consists entirely of evidence which was available at the time of death. We had testimony from two gentlemen who were elected to the positions of authority, Mr. Silvia and Sheriff Fred Robinson. Either of those gentlemen could have overridden, if they saw fit, the decisions made by their predecessors in office.

"I would submit that the timing of this case is directly and entirely attributable to one irrelevant thing. This is the second half of a tautology. The first half was Mrs. Truesdale was guilty of killing Mr. Truesdale because of what happened to Mr. Beasley. The second half is because of what happened to Mr. Truesdale, she is guilty of killing Mr. Beasley. This is bootstrapping at its most sophistry, at the highest degree of sophistry. There is no basis to have waited twenty-seven years. There has been no new evidence. People have testified that they don't remember again and again.

"As you will see in *United States v. Marion*, the Supreme Court has said, 'People should not be called upon to defend stale claims.' This claim is beyond stale, it is beyond rotten. This claim is fully skeletonized."

FitzSimmons was not only eloquent with his dissertation but also dramatically convincing. If the jury was present, he might have won them over. Justice countered with a factual reference of his own: "We contend that the prevailing law on this is *Jones vs. Virginia*, decided by the fourth circuit earlier in the year. It basically says there must be showing of an actual prejudice and the burden to show that is on the defense. All that counsel for the defense has said has been speculative."

FitzSimmons wasn't finished. He got an opportunity to reply: "There is no question but that all of that evidence, together with the solicitor's asserted lack of investigation, was all there in 1967, or perhaps 1974 when a new sheriff came in power, or perhaps 1976 when a new coroner came in power, or perhaps 1976 when Kenny Goode, loyal explorer Scout, returned to Winnsboro to practice law, or Richard Bane, a police officer in another jurisdiction who could exercise some influence from without in the system rather than from within a system they could have us believe was so corrupt and so inept that it didn't see this.

"New evidence comes to light? No. The only thing that came to light is and irrelevant and highly prejudicial event that happened twenty years later in another state."

Once again, FitzSimmons's delivery was extraordinary. His oration could endear a jury, but Rushing wasn't swayed. The judge delivered the defense another crushing blow: "I have tried to examine the prejudice that you argue in this case as to the actual prejudice. It seems to me that the most prejudice in this case was upon the state. The state had the people who were out there done what we believe should have been done today, we may have had a firearms examination, we may have had removal of bullet, comparisons to the weapon, we could have had paraffin tests possibly from the hands of all the parties, of the decedent as well as the accused. We would have had someone talking to these people for the first time and we know were never talked to and who were very obvious, people who were in the home. The court denies the motion to dismiss."

FitzSimmons was shaken. The court denied his motion in a somewhat speculative manner. Rushing referenced today what might have taken place thirty years ago. It was strictly assumption and maybe he could formulate it as a basis for appeal. That was months away. For the moment, he had some fifteen minutes to prepare his closing argument to the jury. It was his final chance for a victory.

27

JOHN JUSTICE'S RIVETING PRESENTATION

The state was the first to present the final summation before the jury. After a ten-minute recess, Justice stood before the jury nearing the lunch hour at approximately 11:25 a.m. Leaving nothing that would disrupt the trial, which was functioning smoothly and rapidly, Rushing made it a point to have lunch ordered for the jury members. There wasn't a thing he missed in orchestrating his concerto. Only after he cautioned the jury that what they were about to hear from the solicitor and the defense attorney was not evidence, was Justice allowed to speak.

"The state must prove that Frances Truesdale, also known as Sandra Beasley, in fact shot and killed her husband, Ronald 'Red' Beasley. I submit to you we have done that. This occurred twenty-nine years ago. The reason it was not prosecuted then is very simply that the defendant was able to convince everyone involved that her husband committed suicide, beginning not the 6th of July, but beginning on the 1st of July. The incident on the 1st of July when Ms. McGinnis woke up and heard moaning coming from Red's bedroom and was intercepted by Sandra, who tells her, 'Don't go in there. Red has tried to kill himself.'

"That was the first murder attempt. Had Betty Ruth McGinnis not awakened, that would have been the murder, because Red Beasley would have lay there and bled to death. But Betty Ruth waking up required Sandra to call an ambulance. Sandra had failed to kill Little Red that morning, but she had very successfully laid the groundwork for killing him six days later.

"He couldn't hold a glass, couldn't hold a spoon. That was the condition he was in. That is the condition he was in the following Thursday morning when Sandra Beasley decides to finish what she had started. And Little Red's father said he heard Sandra say, 'I'm not going to clean up this mess all my life.' And it is obvious that Sandra had set her cap for a new man, a man she married just over a month after she buried her husband.

"Knowing now for sure that she could get away with murder, that people would again believe her story, she very quickly put the plan in motion. This time make sure she finished the job—no more waiting for him to bleed to death—put a bullet in his brain and end this quickly.

"There are some questions I can't answer. Did she move the body after she shot him? Surely, Red Beasley could not blow his brains out and then change the direction and position of his body. She must have moved the body for some reason I do not know.

"If you want to shed a tear for somebody or light a candle or say a prayer, don't do it for Frances Truesdale or Sandra Beasley, do it for Ronald Beasley, who despite his condition, was a human life. That is the person for whom we need to shed a tear, say a prayer or light a candle, not the person who was partying the day he was buried."

Justice was compelling. He minced no words and wisely spoke on the jury's level. No fancy words, nothing but plain and simple lexicon in a homespun manner. It would be all FitzSimmons could do to even match what Justice had delivered. But he positioned himself to be the last one to gain the jury's attention. And they were the ones that mattered. Despite all the court setbacks on his motions, it was the jury who would decide if his client was innocent. He had to reach them for the last time.

It was Fitzsimmons's turn.

"Come listen to the story about a boy named Red. Ladies and gentlemen, I'm sorry to have to do that because I think that is an insult to Red Beasley. I think this entire trial has been an insult to Red Beasley and to his memory. The story you have heard is a story that provokes and begs the question: What? Didn't they have policemen in Winnsboro in 1967? What? Didn't they have a coroner. What? Didn't anybody do his job? What? Didn't the people of Winnsboro care?

"You never heard a single law enforcement agent, officer or personnel say that they investigated this case, and based on their investigation this case was going forward. Sheriff Fred Robinson, who went on to become sheriff in 1974, was there. He said specifically, 'If it had been anything outrageous, I would have written it down.'

"Then there was ambulance driver Julius Cameron. He said that as an adult and a member of this community, a caring member of Fairfield County and society, that he wouldn't hesitate to contact law enforcement if he had seen anything.

"Then there was Ms. Helen Edwards, the records custodian from the hospital. She brought records. And what did she say? She read it aloud. 'He tried to take his life.'

"Then there was Ms. McGinnis. She said Red could feed himself if you gave him small pieces. She lived there. Why would you bother to hand it to him instead of just putting it in his mouth unless it was clear he wanted it in his hand? He exhibited a will to feed himself. And an ability.

"Ms. Caldwell was there fairly often. She testified that Ms. Beasley had blood on her shorts. I don't think there is anything odd about a woman whose husband has just shot himself when she finds him to try and cradle his head as it bleeds in her lap.

"Ladies and gentlemen, we know George Washington was president because somebody wrote it down. There may be someone alive today who says, 'I don't remember it that way.' What was written down in the coroner's report, what was written down in the doctor's reports? It was written down that Red had full use of his left side, partial use of his right side and it was written down in the coroner's report that Red shot himself, that he committed suicide. How do we know the past? People write it down. We rely on written records.

"You can choose your theory, you can acquit my client, Frances Truesdale, because the state has not provided enough evidence to prove her guilt, because the state has waited too long. The evidence has crumbled, people have forgotten and witnesses have died."

FitzSimmons wasn't finished. It may have appeared that way for the moment. Instead, he picked up a toy gun to enlighten the jury, who were about to witness a demonstration FitzSimmons believed would make a lasting impression on them.

"What I am about to show you is not evidence. The judge will instruct you it is not evidence. You cannot consider it as evidence. But I would suggest to you, with my right hand in my pocket, I can pick up with my good left hand, and I am right-handed, this gun.

"This gun is a shooting gallery gun. It shoots cork that you see sticking out on the end of it. It is not cocked. It is not a child's toy. It is sold to be used in shooting galleries that is scaled for an adult to use.

"If I were seated using my left hand and my good left knee, I could press the gun towards my right knee. I could reach with my left hand, without any difficulty, to where the trigger is, and struggling a little because I wouldn't have very good control, I could reach down and get the barrel into my mouth. I believe the evidence is clear."

It was also clear why FitzSimmons purposely wanted to be the last to address the jury. His effective demonstration wouldn't allow any confutation by Justice. It was a strategic ploy he cultivated even before the trial began. Rushing adjourned the court until 2:30 p.m. after getting both attorneys to agree on the exhibits.

Through it all, Sandra sat there motionless, almost lifeless trapped like a myopic butterfly in a spider's nest. Her eyes had always been riveted on the witness stand, where one by one the solicitor's subjects had appeared, recounting what they thought happened thirty years ago. How could they distort the accounts, she thought to herself. Some she felt even lied. She was the only person who could dispute them, yet she couldn't utter a word. If she had agreed to take the stand in her own defense, it would expose her to the sentence she was currently serving for the murder of Jerry Truesdale in 1988. She was a prisoner of herself.

Sandra appeared emotionless for the third straight day and apparently resigned to her fate of a second murder verdict of guilty. The odds of her acquittal were narrow. There were too many witnesses who went unchallenged, and she fully realized it was damaging to her defense. Yet she honestly felt she would have been exonerated—otherwise she wouldn't have waived extradition to stand trial in the first place. Given the circumstances, her defense did an exceptional performance. They had little to go on, yet the telling lack of evidence that FitzSimmons brought to the attention of the jury manifested doubt.

How could they reach a guilty verdict when there was reasonable doubt substantiated by a doctor's admission that Ron Beasley actually walked with a hospital orderly's help? Or even the dramatic demonstration FitzSimmons produced in revealing that even a paraplegic could easily pull the trigger of a .22 rifle. And as FitzSimmons stressed so often, no new evidence was introduced and no murder weapon was recovered. There was even an investigative officer at the crime scene who couldn't remember seeing the body of Ron Beasley or even what year he was elected sheriff, and how many of the state's witnesses experienced difficulty in recalling what actually happened?

Sandra's fate was completely in the minds of the jury. When they returned from recess, they asked the court for review of the testimony of McGinnis. After it was played back, the jury retired to the jury room at 4:15 p.m. to continue deliberating even for them a most unusual case. An hour and a half later, they indicated that they had agreed on a verdict. But before they returned to render it, Rushing addressed the court in the manner he displayed throughout the trial, specifically, the courtroom was his domain and he would conduct its affairs his way. He looked right at the audience.

"For those of you who are family, friends, whatever, I don't permit any expression of happiness or disappointment in the verdict of the jury, sighs, clapping or otherwise. That is improper. We ask these people to decide these cases and to allow such conduct would be improper and not in respect of their responsibilities as well.

"If you cannot handle the verdict of the jury, you may leave. If I hear any response, I am going to direct that you be held in contempt of court right then. I am going to place you in jail. So, don't do it. I have warned you and that is the only chance you are going to get."

At 5:45 p.m., the jury foreman handed the written verdict to the clerk, who presented it to Rushing. He examined it and ordered the clerk to announce the verdict.

"Guilty."

Sandra heard the word for the second time. She seemed immune and never moved or even sighed. She remained solemn and briefly compressed her lips, remorseful that she ever returned to Winnsboro to gain an acquittal, which would allow her a basis for an appeal in the second-degree murder charge of Jerry Truesdale.

After the jury was released, Rushing pronounced sentence. Under the law in 1967, Sandra's conviction carried a life sentence. Since then, the law was changed to read thirty years to life. It specified that Sandra must remain incarcerated for 85 percent of her sentence before being eligible for parole after five years. Rushing offered the right to appeal. It was all she could take away from the courtroom.

Accompanied by a bailiff, Sandra left the courtroom to a cell just to the left of the chamber door to await a final meeting with her attorney. When Rushing sounded his gavel, officially ending the trial, family members and friends approached Justice with all the platitudes reserved for heroes. Their elation was visible by repetitious handshakes and thank-yous. The overriding mood was relief as Ann Letrick wiped the tears from her eyes.

The scene was like déjà vu for Jody Truesdale. Just five years earlier, he watched in disbelief as a Roanoke jury convicted his mother of murdering his stepfather. He was consoled by his wife, who had her arm around his waist. There was nothing left for him to do now except to return to his two daughters in Winston-Salem with the thought that one day when they are grown, he would have to explain to them about their grandmother.

"He was the only daddy I ever knew," remarked Jody about Jerry Truesdale. "And now, it hurts to think that she took two fathers away from me."

Letrick had always believed that if the authorities had done their job thirty years ago, her brother would still be alive today. The guilty verdict that Sandra received now was only bittersweet.

"I'm not the happiest person in the world because my brother isn't here," sighed Ann. "But I'm glad Sandra's getting what she deserves. The main thing is that I can have closure now. When they said 'guilty,' I felt like a hundred pounds had been lifted off my heart."

Ron Beasley's aunt Claudine Humphries was one of three sisters and two brothers who gave support to Pop Beasley by appearing every day at the trial. She was realistic at its conclusion.

"It can't be a happy ending because there are five children involved," she pointed out. "It's just closure."

Pop Beasley felt much the same way.

"There's no way I can express any joy, but I'm glad it's over," remarked Pop. "Maybe now we can get our lives together and move on. I just especially hope Jody can go on with his life. This has been hard on him."

There was relief, too, and satisfaction for Young both professionally and personally. Before he took office, the report given to the Fairfield County Sheriff's Office by the Virginia State Police was virtually ignored for two years.

"She's been found guilty and she'll have to pay for it," reasoned Young. "She just never showed any reaction or emotion."

Through the years, Sandra Frances Ann Scott Mitchell Beasley Truesdale has remained a mystery, especially to those who knew her. Sitting alone in a courthouse cell, she presented an even deeper one.

28
CLOSURE

The Fairfield County Detention Center is a squalid one-story facility that looks like an eyesore on Highway 321 By-Pass about two miles from the courthouse in which Frances Truesdale received a thirty-year sentence for murder. While modern prison facilities are being built for a nation with a rising crime rate, the Fairfield County Detention Center remains a relic of the past. It is far removed from modern-day penal institutions, sitting on top of a bumpy gravel and dirt road that yearns for anonymity.

It is a dimly lit old square building with concrete floors, with most of the illumination centering over the desk sergeant's area to the left of the entrance, protected from the outside by a silver-painted iron gate that is secured to the floor and doesn't stop until it reaches the ceiling. There are not many portals that offer daylight, yet the place remains clean and somewhat tidy with the presence of starched white-shirted security guards.

This was Frances Truesdale's living quarters, sharing a cell with a couple of other inmates, quite different from the living conditions she enjoyed at the Virginia Women's Correctional Institution the last four years. There she was a model prisoner, and with it came the amenities of a room of her own with a window, nothing resembling the desultory atmosphere of a prison cell in Winnsboro that most inhabitants would find debilitating. Ironically, this is where it all began for Frances thirty years ago in another part of town, a housewife with four little boys living in a house on a knoll on Forest Hills Drive.

Just one day after a Winnsboro jury found her guilty of Ron Beasley's murder, Frances appeared irate while puffing on still another cigarette, her head leaning against a brick wall. It wasn't the verdict that bothered her as much as the suicide watch she was subjected to throughout the night. She felt the night-long surveillance was an affront, one that left her awake for most of the night after a traumatic day in court.

A model inmate, she laughed out loud at being under a death watch. She slept with the light on in her cell, and every twenty minutes a benevolent guard would peer into her cubicle to see if she was still alive. She was ready for them. She smiled and waved each time, even chiding one for being late for one of the twenty-minute intervals. Often, lying on her bed, she would extend her arms upward to show that she wasn't hiding anything that could take her life.

"I was brought here from Virginia classified as no security risk," pointed out Frances while cradling her legs underneath her. "There was no recommendation by the Virginia authorities. I had been up there for four and a half years without any infractions whatsoever which earned me a single, private room. This was too much."

It was during that sleepless night that Frances thought about the trial. She could see all the witnesses that appeared those two days just as clearly as if she was sitting in the courtroom. How could they testify the way that they did, Betty McGinnis, Mattie Caldwell, Pop Beasley, Herman Young and Kenny Goode, leaving her defenseless for a jury to decide her fate? "Lies, all lies," she repeated to herself through the restless night.

She wondered why her attorney didn't hammer home the point that Ron could walk and, in fact, did walk. It was all there on the medical report, in black and white, on his discharge papers from Fairfield Memorial Hospital. "Patient was able to walk with the aid of an orderly," wrote the discharging doctor. She said Ron could walk, and the doctor confirmed it. Why didn't anyone believe her? The testimony of what took place thirty years ago was strictly hearsay, no evidence, no eyewitnesses, nothing. Why did they wait so long to come forward with fragmented memories? But that hospital report said it all: Ron Beasley walked.

The more she was awake, the more what took place thirty years ago became clearer. The party, the night of Ron's funeral. What party? Frances had no memory of it. But she couldn't take the stand in her own defense to tell her own story of what had happened.

"Dr. Floyd's nurse gave me a shot and put me to bed after the funeral but nobody mentioned that," swore Frances, her eyes bulging with disbelief.

"The family was meeting at the Beasleys' because I was incoherent and they didn't want anybody around me. Betty Ruth was there, and so was her mother, sitting in the Beasley house that was lined up with funeral chairs.

"I was incoherent the day before with the same shot that Dr. Floyd ordered. I was told later, after I had awakened, that the funeral arrangements had already been made. Barbara Bane, Ron's sister, told me she had made them. There was nothing for me to do.

"I love Pop Beasley. He never had a harsh word or criticized me until I was imprisoned in Virginia. I had no contact with him since then. I looked at him on the witness stand and saw how frail he had become and I felt so sorry for him.

"What he said was out of context of a conversation, an argument, really, one in the driveway after Ron suffered his stroke. I was a nervous wreck after a month, frantic, overworked, twenty-four years old and scared to death of all that was happening around me. I said, 'I can't keep picking up after Ron the rest of my life. I can't do it by myself. I have to have help. I want my kids back home with me and I can't do it all. I'll drop dead in my tracks doing all this by myself. I can't keep up the pace.' And, he and Mom Beasley agreed on the spot that they would pay Mattie.

"The day that Ron died, the coroner, Earl Boulware, talked to Mattie, which she never mentioned. He talked to me and Pop, too. He asked both of us if we thought an inquest was necessary. And Pop told him no. Pop has always showed me compassion, understanding and love. There were many times he hugged my neck in the last twenty years that I know it was love. There was no hate, no suspicions."

Twice a year Frances and Jerry would drive from Winston-Salem to Winnsboro, bringing Jody with them to visit his grandfather. Pop Beasley was extremely fond of Jody, who was in Pop's eyes an extension of his father. When Jody got older, he would spend a couple of weeks in the summer with Mom and Pop Beasley.

"Jody always knew the connection of him with the Beasleys, even as a child," said Frances, holding back tears. "He had a bedroom in the house that was his father's. The room was filled with pictures of Ron and Jody was always told that Ron was his first daddy."

But now, when Frances wanted to see him most, so much so that her eyes reddened, there was no Jody. Whatever had happened during this endless nightmare, she was still his mother. She gave him birth, raised and loved him, and no one can say that she failed as a mother. She just wanted to touch him, talk to him, one more time. It left her empty almost to the point of despair.

If there was any redeeming quality that identified Frances, it was the love of her children, which appeared as a beacon in a cold and barren detention cell. That's all she had left now, and even the thought of returning to her model prisoner status in Goochland the next day didn't ease her pain.

"I'm right with God," she remarked in parting.

The small beige house on Forest Hills Drive is hauntingly empty now, lifeless from neglect. It has been unoccupied for a number of years, perhaps burdened by a curse of a house that was alive with a man and his wife and four small children. It is the monument Ron Beasley left behind with a mysterious secret: did he, or could he, have killed himself?

It was a fall like no other in Winnsboro. Richard Winn completed an unprecedented second straight Class A football season at 12-0 that brought a second consecutive state championship; across town, Fairfield Central erupted into a Class AAA power and a state championship with a 13-0 record; Sheriff Herman Young was reelected to his office with a resounding victory over Wayne Yates; Tim Wilkes ran unopposed for the state legislature; Strom Thurmond was successful in his reelection bid for the U.S. Senate for an eighth term and became the most enduring figure in American politics at the age of ninety-three; Johnny Porter harvested his field of cotton in what seemed like an endless summer; and finally, Frances Truesdale returned to the town where she was known as Sandra Beasley and was found guilty of murdering her husband in 1967. Only she, and she alone, knew how he died.

"I'm right with God," she repeated as the chain door closed behind her.

Frances disappeared into a long corridor and with her took the secret of two mysterious deaths. At that lonely moment, it was closure.

SOURCES

Greenville News
Herald Independent
LA Times
Newberry Observer
Orlando Sentinel
The State

ABOUT THE AUTHOR

A prolific author, Lou Sahadi has written twenty-eight major books, among them the official autobiographies of Willie Mays, Don Shula, Len Dawson, Hank Stram and an intimate biography of Johnny Unitas, which has been optioned for a movie. His book *The Long Pass* was selected for inclusion in the Nixon Presidential Library.

He has been a contributor and interviewee of the *New York Times*, the *New York Post*, *Miami Herald*, *The State*, the *Sun Sentinel*, *Greenville Journal*, *Gear*, *US Weekly* and others. In addition, he has made appearances on CNN and ESPN as well as local TV and radio stations.

Sahadi's latest book, *The Last Triple Crown* (St. Martin's Press), received excellent reviews: "One of the greatest racing rivalries of all times deserves an equally world class story teller to make it come alive so many years later. Mr. Sahadi gets you so close to the action, you can almost smell the hay in the stalls of these two equine super stars," wrote Leonard Shapiro in the *Washington Post*.

Also by the Author

The Long Pass (World Books; Bantam Paperback)
Miracle in Miami (Henry Regnery Books)
Pro Football's Gamebreakers (Contemporary Books)
Broncos! (Stein & Day)
Super Sundays I-XII (Contemporary Books)
Year of the Yankees (Contemporary Books)
Steelers: Team of the Decade (New York Times Books)
Super Steelers (New York Times Books)
The Pirates (New York Times Books)
Super Sunday's XV (Contemporary Books)
The Raiders (Dial Press)
Super Sunday's XVI (Contemporary Books)
L.A. Dodgers (William Morrow)
The 49ers (William Morrow)
The Clemson Tigers: From 1896 to Glory (William Morrow)
The Redskins (William Morrow)
Johnny Unitas: America's Quarterback (Triumph Books)
One Sunday in December (Lyons Press)
Affirmed…The Last Triple Crown (St. Martins Press)
100 Things Clemson Fans Should Know & Do Before They Die (Triumph Books)

Biographies

Len Dawson: Pressure Quarterback (Cowles Books) by Len Dawson with Lou Sahadi
The Winning Edge (EP Dutton; Popular Library Paperback) by Don Shula with Lou Sahadi
They're Playing My Game (William Morrow; St. Martins Paperback) by Hank Stram with Lou Sahadi
Say Hey! (Simon & Schuster; Pocketbook Paperback) by Willie Mays with Lou Sahadi
Winning My Way (Tiger Press) by Jim Donnan with Lou Sahadi
They're Playing My Game (Revised-Triumph Books) by Hank Stram with Lou Sahadi

Television

Remembering Marshall (ESPN; November 2001)